150 SOLITAIRE GAMES

150 SOLITAIRE GAMES

DOUGLAS BROWN

PERENNIAL LIBRARY

Harper & Row, Publishers, New York
Grand Rapids, Philadelphia, St. Louis, San Francisco
London, Singapore, Sydney, Tokyo, Toronto

The book was originally published by Ottenheimer Publishers, Inc. in 1966 under the title *The Key to Solitaire*. It is here reprinted by arrangement with Ottenheimer Publishers, Inc.

First Perennial Library edition published 1985.

Library of Congress Cataloging in Publication Data

150 solitaire games.

Reprint. Originally published: The key to solitaire. Baltimore : Ottenheimer, 1966.

1. Solitaire (Game)   I. Title.   II. Title: One hundred fifty solitaire games.

GV1261.G53   1985   795.4'3   84-48140

ISBN 0-06-092315-6

---

96 97 98 99 RRD 20 19 18 17 16 15 14 13 12

CONTENTS

150 SOLITAIRE GAMES

SOLITAIRE EXPLAINED

In games of Patience or Solitaire, cards are considered according to the following terms:

Values: As in most card games, Ace, Two, Three and so on, including the picture cards, Jack, Queen, King.

Suits: consisting of Clubs, Diamonds, Hearts, Spades.

Colors: of which there are two, Red and Black.

Some games use a regular pack of 52 cards, while others need a double pack. For convenience, these are given in different sections, but the style is much the same in both. In all games, cards are dealt in some special arrangement. This is called:

The Tableau: consists of single cards, groups, piles, which have their own purposes and limitations, as described in each game.

Foundations: are cards upon which others are built to form complete sequences, thus terminating the game. The Foundations may be part of the original Tableau, or they may be established during play, according to the individual game.

Ascending Sequences: run from a low card, usually an Ace, on up to the high card, as A, 2, 3, 4, 5, 6, 7, 8, 9, 10, J, Q, K.

Decending Sequences: run from a high card, usually a King, on down to the low card, as K, Q, J, 10, 9, 8, 7, 6, 5, 4, 3, 2, A.

Auxiliary Cards: belong to the Tableau, which may be built upon Foundations, or may be used for forming temporary sequences, according to the rules.

Rows: are cards dealt crosswise in the Tableau, either singly or overlapping, as specified.

Columns: are cards dealt vertically in the Tableau, either singly or overlapping, as specified.

The Stock: is a term applied to the remainder of

the pack after the Tableau has been arranged.

The Reserve: is a packet or group of cards that is laid aside or specially retained for building on Foundations.

Available Cards: are any that are free for building on foundations, or for transfer to auxiliary cards or columns.

Blocked Cards: are those which must in some way be released to become available.

The Waste Pile: consists of cards that can not be used when dealt and therefore must be laid aside. Some games are lost when all the stock has gone into the waste pile. Others allow the waste pile to be used as a new stock, as specified in the rules of individual games.

Other terms will be mentioned whenever needed in descriptions of individual games, along with the application of the terms already given.

Simple Pairs

This game, as its name implies, is simple to play and therefore requires a very simple tableau. As illustrated, the tableau consists of nine cards dealt in three rows, each, forming a square.

Values only are considered and there are no foundations, so nothing is built. All you do is weed out pairs from the tableau, leaving open spaces. These are filled with fresh cards from the pack and the pairing is continued. The whole idea is to pair out the entire pack.

Only pairs count; no trios. Where there are three cards alike — as with the Aces shown in the illustrated tableau — only two may be removed as a pair. The odd card must stay until another is dealt to match it. Of course, if all four of a value are showing at once, they may be removed as two pairs.

SIMPLE PAIRS

In the illustrated tableau, three pairs can be removed: Two Aces, two Fives and two Jacks. That leaves only three cards in the tableau, so six more are dealt to fill. With a start like that, the game should be dead easy, but don't be sure of that. Even though there are only thirteen values, with nine cards to pick from, there are times when the deal winds up with the cards in the tableau all different, which may be very early in the deal.

To allow for that, a special rule has been introduced, letting the player turn up an extra card, shown dotted in the illustrated tableau. He can only do this when he finds it impossible to pair up two cards from the square itself. If the extra can be paired with one of the cards in the square, that is done and the game continues. If the extra won't pair up, the game is lost.

If the extra does pair up, there will be one space in the square, so a single card is dealt to fill it. If that won't pair, the player can again deal an extra card just as he did before. When working with an odd card like that, the game becomes exciting. If you have a pack containing two Jokers, keep them in it and count them as an extra pair, making the game that much harder.

When the whole pack gets down to ten cards — nine in the square and one extra — victory is assured, so that is really the player's goal. From that point, he simply pairs off all that remain. This makes a good two player game, each with his own pack, each trying to pair off more cards than the other.

Canfield

The tableau is formed by dealing a horizontal row of seven cards from left to right, the first card face up, becoming Column 1, and the rest face down. A row of six cards is then dealt from left to right, beginning with Column 2, the first face up, and the rest face down. This is repeated with a row of five cards, beginning with Column 3, and so on.

All columns are dealt so that the cards overlap, with the result that there are seven columns containing from one to seven cards in that order, and the card at the foot of each column is face up and available. The rest of the pack is used as a stock and is kept face down.

Any available Aces are removed from their columns and placed in a row as foundations. Any Two can be placed on an Ace of the same suit clear up to Kings. Whenever a card is taken from a column, the card then at the foot is turned face up and becomes available.

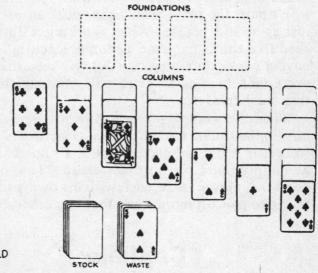

CANFIELD

STOCK   WASTE

Such cards may be transferred from column to column, if they form descending sequences in opposite colors. A black Six can be put on a red Seven, a red Five may then be put on the black Six, and so on down. Such sequences should also overlap, because each can only be transferred as a group, never card by card.

A sequence formed with Red Seven, Black Six, Red Five, could be put on a Black Eight in another column. But in building on to a foundation, the card at the bottom of the column is still used, and no other. Such a sequence as 7H, 6C, 5D could be put on the 8C or 8S, but meanwhile the 5D could be built on the 4D in a foundation pile. That would make the 6C available to be built on the 5C, and so on.

Lucky Thirteen

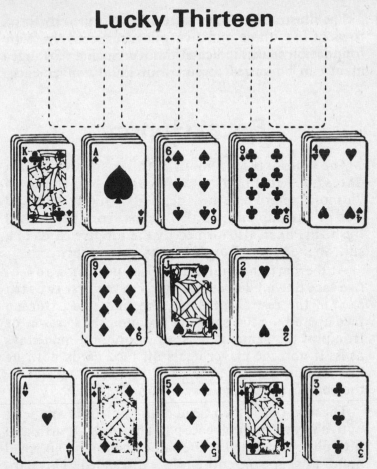

The thirteen visible cards are immediately available for play. Any Aces among them are set aside in a separate row, to serve as foundations, on which cards of the same suit are built in ascending sequence, Ace to King, the purpose of the game being to complete all such builds.

Cards can also be transferred from one auxiliary pile to another. This is done in descending sequence, from King down to Ace, and in such transfers, suits do not matter. But only the top card of each pile can be transferred, so if an Eight is put on a Nine and a Seven put on the Eight, only the Seven can be moved later.

The illustration shows the tableau formed by three rows of five, three and five piles, respectively, with foundation spaces indicated above. Such an arrangement can be varied to suit individual convenience.

Royal Honors

The tableau is continuous in this fast game, which dates back to the days of Whist, when the term "honors" referred to the Ace, King, Queen, Jack and Ten of a trump suit. It also stems from the "royal flush" in Poker, also formed by the top five cards of a suit. So the name "Royal Honors" fits doubly.

At the start, the shuffled pack is dealt in a row of five face down piles, eleven cards in the first two; ten each in the rest. That done, the first pile is turned face up and the suit showing becomes the key suit or trump of the game. If it is an honor, the pile stays as is. If not, the player deals off face cards until he hits an honor of that suit. The pile then stays as is, the dealt cards being thrown from the game.

The next pile is then turned up and cards are dealt until a royal honor is reached. The third, fourth and fifth piles are treated in the same fashion. If no royal honor appears, the entire pile is discarded. This happens whenever there is more than one honor in the same pile.

Now, the piles are gathered, the fifth going on the fourth, fourth on third, third on second, second on first. If any piles are gone, the space is jumped when gathering the rest. The packet is turned face down as a new stock, which is dealt off until a royal honor is reached, blank piles again being eliminated.

The piles are gathered, 4, 3, 2, 1 and turned face down; three piles are dealt, processed, and gathered 3, 2, 1. Then two piles are dealt, treated as before and gathered to form a single pile, provided the game goes that far. In all cases, the cards are dealt singly, pile by pile.

The purpose is to bring all the royal honors together in one pile, with no other cards whatever. If this happens before the final deal, the game is won then and there. Generally, it narrows down to two piles and if all waste cards can be eliminated from both, they can be gathered to show royal honors only.

Sometimes one or two sandwiched cards can spoil this happy climax and the game must be given up. But if the first pile shows one or more honors with odd cards beneath, and the second pile is all honors, the player may put the second pile on the first, turn the packet face down and deal a single pile. When this is turned face up, the waste cards will be uppermost and can therefore be thrown out, scoring a win.

The illustrated tableau shows the five piles as orig-

inally dealt. (Diagram A) The second illustration
shows how they might appear when turned up. (Diagram B) The third illustration shows the result of
the discarding process, with the piles ready to be
gathered from right to left. (Diagram C)

Poker Solitaire

The tableau requires twenty-five cards, dealt at
random from the pack, forming five rows of five
cards each. From there on, it is entirely different
from any other form of solitaire. The purpose of the
game is to arrange the cross rows, so that each forms
a perfect poker hand, with no left-over cards.

Poker hands or combinations run as follows:

Straight Flush: Five cards of one suit in sequence,
as Ten, Nine, Eight, Seven, Six of Diamonds.

Four of a Kind: Four cards of the same value,
with any odd card, as four Kings with an extra like
an Eight of Clubs.

Full House: Three of one value, two of another,
as three Eights with two Sixes.

Flush: Five cards of the same suit, not in sequence.

Straight: Five cards in sequence but not of one suit.

All the above named are "pat hands" which
means they are perfect in the sense that they can not
be improved, without destroying their present status. This applies to Four of a Kind as much as the
others, because the odd card does not affect it in
any way. Only such hands are considered in Poker
Solitaire. Lesser combinations (Three of a Kind,
Two Pair) are not "pat" hands.

At first sight, it may seem impossible to make perfect Poker hands out of a random mixture of twenty-
five cards. But it can be done many times in many
ways, and some persons are so skilled that they sel-

dom fail. It may mean switching combinations when the game seems almost completed, but persistency usually wins.

START

POKER SOLITAIRE

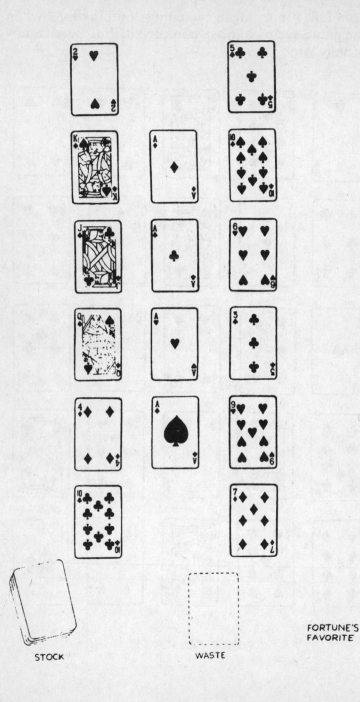

STOCK   WASTE   FORTUNE'S
                                         FAVORITE

Full House (K-K-K-3-3)
Straight(10-9-8-7-6)
Flush (All Hearts)
Flush (All Spades)
Four of a Kind (Aces with odd Queen)

In many cases, Flushes are the easiest combinations to form, as there are sure to be five or more cards in at least two different suits, and usually there are three suits that offer possible Flushes. But sometimes a sure Flush must be sacrificed to make up another hand, which adds to the interest of this game.

Fortune's Favorite

To form the tableau, place the four Aces in a column, alternating red and black. Shuffle the pack and deal two columns of six cards each, to left and right of the Aces.

The Aces are the foundations, to be built up to Kings, with cards of the same suit. The left and right columns are separate auxiliary cards, which may become packets as play proceeds.

The stock, or remainder of the pack is laid face down in readiness.

Play proceeds as follows: Any available cards are built on the foundations, if suitable. Otherwise, any available cards may be moved from one auxiliary packet to another, provided they are in descending sequence in the same suit.

Following such builds or transfers, cards may be turned up on the stock, one by one. These may be used to build on Foundations or placed on auxiliary packets in descending sequence, if suitable. Otherwise, they may be used to fill spaces formed by moving cards in the tableau.

In the illustrated tableau, the 2H can be built on the A H. The Q S can be transferred to the K S. The 10C can be transferred to the J C. This leaves three spaces in the tableau to be filled.

If one of those should be the 4C, it could be placed on the 5C instead of filling a space. If the 2C should be dealt shortly afterward, it could be built on the A C, followed by the 3C, 4C, 5C.

This game, though an easy type, may run into bad blocks, making it hard to work back through the waste pile. A second deal is allowed on that account. When the stock is used up, the waste pile is turned face down and dealt as a new stock.

Tam O'Shanter

The tableau for this game is very simple, four cards being dealt from a shuffled pack to form a face up row. But the player allows room for four foundation piles to be placed beyond the four auxiliaries as dealt. This is shown in the illustrated tableau. (A)

The Aces are used as foundations, so if any appear in the original tableau, they are removed and placed in their proper area. Building is in ascending sequence, Ace up to King, but values alone are considered; not suits.

In the illustrated tableau, an Ace and Two both appear, so they would be built accordingly, leaving only two cards in the auxiliary row. This is shown in the second illustration. (Diagram B)

Another row of four auxiliary cards is dealt upon the first, and again any possible builds are made from the auxiliary row to the foundations. But here a strict rule is invoked that often makes the game difficult. No cards can be built from the auxiliary row until its four new cards have been dealt.

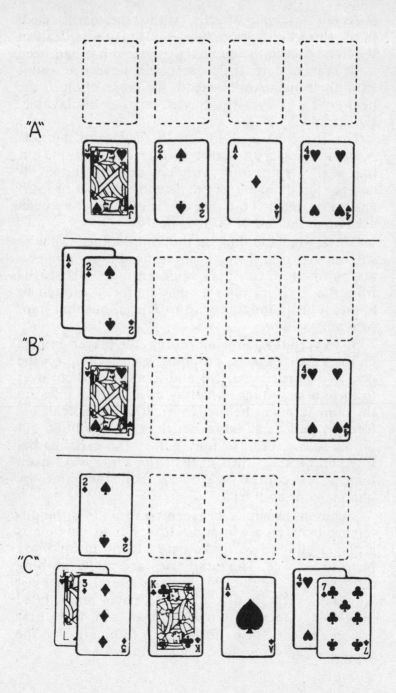

As an example of this, study the cards dealt
in the third illustration. There, a Three was dealt in
the first space in the auxiliary row, and if it had been
built immediately, the Four could have been built
from the fourth row. Instead, the completion of the
deal covers it with the Seven, so it is unplayable.
(Diagram C)

The Three can be built on the Two and the new
Ace can be placed to start another foundation, but
that is all. Again, four cards are dealt in the auxiliary row on the same terms; then another set of four,
and so on until the entire pack of cards has been
used up at the end of thirteen deals.

Often, when building on the foundations, a player
will uncover a card which can be used in an immediate build. If he can play back enough such cards
from the auxiliary piles he may be lucky enough to
build all his foundations up to Kings, but that happens very seldom.

So to keep the game interesting, the player gathers
up the auxiliary piles, dropping each face up on the
next in the order, 4, 3, 2, 1 and then turns them over
to form a new stock, which is dealt in four piles on
the same terms as before, four cards being dealt before any builds can be made. If he fails to build out
on the second deal, he may gather the cards as before and make a third deal in the same way. Even
then, a few contrary cards can ruin the game, by
blocking one another.

Sometimes a choice between two builds is the difference between a win and a loss, but at no time is
a player allowed to move cards from an auxiliary
heap to a space. The auxiliaries are really nothing
more than waste piles in this game, and each must
stay as is, except for direct builds. Spaces can be filled
only by the regular four card deal from the stock.

Some restrict the builds on each foundation to the
same suit, allowing three deals to the game.

Eleven O'Clock

The tableau is a circle of twelve cards like the face of a clock, but these are dealt at random from a shuffled pack. Spot cards only make up the tableau, any picture cards being returned to the pack, which is again shuffled after the tableau is complete.

There is no building on foundations, nor any waste pile, and cards are considered by value alone, 1 to 10, with the pictures being disregarded. Play is simple: You note any two cards on the tableau that total 11, as a Three and Eight; a Five and Six; an Ace and Ten. On any such pair, you deal two cards from the stock, face up. This is continued, pair after pair, as long as the dial shows two cards that together total 11.

New cards supplant those that they cover, so that new pairs totaling 11 frequently come in view. The game is to use up the entire pack by continuing to cover such pairs. The picture cards do not count, so in the simple form of "Eleven O'Clock" they are dealt to one side as the game proceeds, or they can be removed beforehand so the game is played with a 40 card pack.

That way, the game may become too simple, so it is better to use the picture cards as blockers. Start with number cards only in the tableau, as already mentioned, but if any picture cards appear while pairing elevens, they stay where dealt and block that from further use. This decreases the available piles and the game becomes harder.

Rather than have it too hard, you may use this privilege. When only two number cards show on the dial, as an Eight and a Three, any picture cards that are dealt may be replaced on the bottom of the stock. That leaves a numbered pair still open, another card being dealt instead of the picture card.

That leaves a numbered pair still open, another card being dealt instead of the picture card.

The game still can end at that point, if the next two cards do not total 11. If you dealt a Five and Two on the Eight and Three, it would be impossible to proceed with no other number cards still showing in the tableau.

STOCK

In the tableau illustrated, there are three combinations forming 11, consisting of A-10, 5-6 and 8-3. You could begin by dealing six cards face up on those. If those cards happened to run Two, Jack, Queen, Ten, Eight, King, the game would be blocked immediately. But if they should run Six, Nine, Ace, Nine, Seven, Six, there would be a wealth of combinations totalling 11, waiting for a further deal.

Kings and Queens

The tableau in this game is quite simple. Take the black Kings and the red Queens from the pack and lay them in a row as Foundations. The remainder of the pack is then shuffled and dealt in as many as three heaps, all face up.

The play starts with the dealing of the very first card, provided it can be built on any of the foundations. The building, follows a special rule in this game: On each King, the suit is built upward, K, A, 2, 3, 4, 5, 6, 7, 8, 9, 10, J, Q. This applies to the black suits, Spades and Clubs.

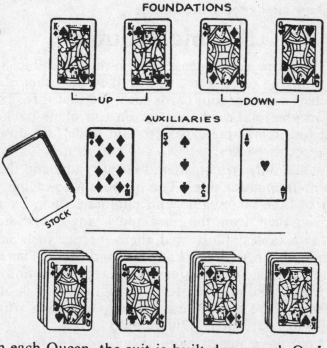

On each Queen, the suit is built downward, Q, J,

10, 9, 8, 7, 6, 5, 4, 3, 2, A, K. This applies to the red suits, Hearts and Diamonds. It is simply a case of ascending sequences with one color; descending sequences with the other.

After the three auxiliary heaps have exhausted the stock, they are gathered in any order and turned face down to become a new stock. From then on, the cards must be dealt from the stock into a single waste pile. These are dealt face up and the top card of the waste pile is always available for building, but the player has less scope than with the auxiliary heaps.

When this deal is finished, the game is ended, unless the player managed to complete his builds before them. That is usually very difficult, as the game does not have much leeway. So most players simply count up the total cards in the foundation piles to see how high a score they made.

Double Trouble

The entire pack is dealt to form the tableau in this fast-moving game. First shuffle the pack, then deal twelve packets of four cards each, the first three face down, the final card face up on top of its packet. The four remaining cards are laid aside face down, as a reserve packet.

Values only are considered in this game and there are no foundation piles. The purpose is to match up pairs of the same value and eliminate them by removing them from the piles and laying them aside.

In the tableau illustrated, there are four such pairs consisting of Aces, Eights, Nines and Jacks. There is a third Eight, which gives the player an option as to which two he wants to remove, though it is only guess-work, since there is no way of telling which will work out better. (Diagram A)

After the matched pairs have been discarded, the new top cards are turned up on the packets. If any

of these can be paired, either with each other, or
with the orginal top cards that still remain, they are
eliminated in the same way. (Diagram B)

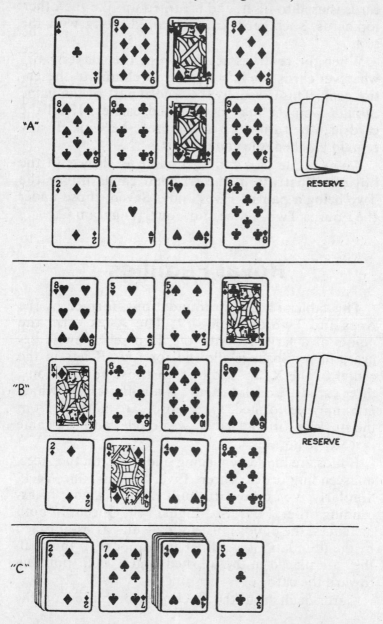

This lets the player turn up more cards on the heaps involved and if new pairs can be matched, that is done. Whenever a space results, one of the reserve cards is used to fill it, and is turned up like the other top cards. Such cards can be paired along with the rest.

When the reserves are used up, the player pairs whatever cards are left, hoping to eliminate the entire pack. This is usually the crucial part of the game though a player may be stopped earlier. If all the cards can be turned up and paired. he wins. If any remain blocked, the game is lost.

An example of a blocked game is shown in the bottom illustration, the trapped cards under the Two being a pair of Fives and a Seven; those under the Four, a Two, Three and Four. (Diagram C.)

Royal Families

This tableau has eight foundations, formed by the Aces and Two of each suit, The Aces form the points of a large X, with the Two set sidewise beneath them. Space is allowed for four Kings in the center of the X. In addition to those foundations, three cards are dealt face up as auxiliaries, on which piles may be formed. One more card is dealt from the stock to form a face up waste pile, and the game is ready to go.

Builds are made by placing odd cards on the Aces, in ascending order, Three, Five, Seven, Nine, Jack. Similarly even cards are built on the Twos, in ascending order, Four, Six, Eight, Ten, Queen. In both instances, the builds must follow suits as established by the foundations. As the Kings appear in the deal, they are placed in the allotted space, each pointing toward the cards of is own suit.

Cards dealt from the stock may be placed on the

auxiliary cards in descending order, odd or even as the case may be, and they must always follow suit, as 7C on 9C, followed by 5C on 7C, or with evens, 10C on Q C, 8C on 10C, etc. Auxiliary cards can be placed on one another, as long as they follow the same rule, and they can also be built on the foundations.

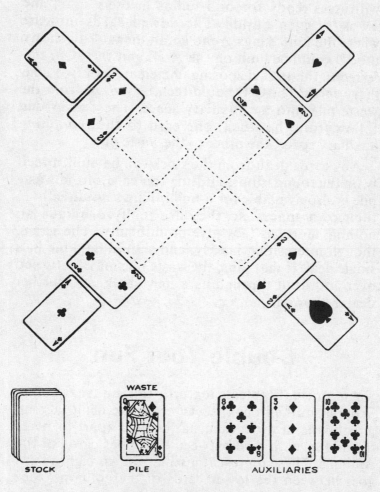

STOCK   PILE   AUXILIARIES

ROYAL FAMILIES

As a result, spaces frequently occur in the auxiliary row, and these can be filled from the stock, or by the card showing on the waste pile. This makes more cards available for building and at the finish, the tableau should consist of the entire pack forming a letter X, with Jacks, Queens and Kings of each suit showing on each arm.

The illustrated tableau shows the start of the game with Aces ready for odd builds in their suits, and Twos for even builds. The dotted cards indicate where the four Kings are to go. In the tableau shown the 3D could be built on the A D, and the 8C transferred to the 10C, disposing immediately of two auxiliary cards. The Q D could then be moved from the waste pile into an auxiliary space. The deal would follow from the stock, one card to the remaining auxiliary space, the other to the waste pile.

Any cards dealt from the stock can be built directly on the foundations, and the top card of the waste pile is also available for a build. Kings go directly in their own spaces, so they are really ornamental, nothing more, as they give no difficulty. The game, though interesting, is easy, and should be done in a single deal. If that fails, the waste pile may be turned over and dealt through as a new stock. No further deal is allowed.

Double Your Fun

An unusual tableau features this unusual game. From a shuffled pack, seven cards are dealt face up in columns of three each, far enough apart to place the odd seventh card between the upper cards of the columns. These represent auxiliaries. An eighth card goes between the lower cards of the columns, face up. It becomes the one and only foundation, which is why the game is unusual.

If any Kings turn up during the deal, they are replaced on the bottom of the pack, for a reason to be
explained. A single card is dealt below as the start of

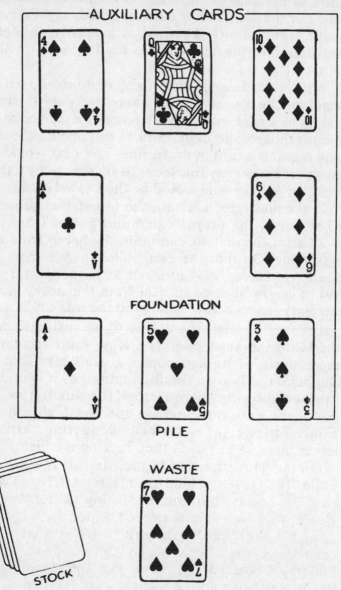

a waste pile, while the stock, or bulk of the pack, is retained in hand, face down.

All is then ready for play, which involves a special form of building on the lone foundation. First. the value of the foundation card is noted, say Five, as value alone counts. Then, it is mentally doubled, and a card of the new value is built upon it, in this case a Ten.

Next, the value of that card is doubled, which would make Twenty. Since there are only thirteen values in a pack (Ace up to King) the player must deduct thirteen. So in place of twenty, he has Seven, and requires a card of that value. The next would be twice seven, namely fourteen, so by subtracting thirteen, an Ace (or one) would be the needed card.

In the illustrated tableau, the foundation shows a Five. On it, the player can build a Ten from the auxiliaries. On that, he can build the Seven from the waste pile. On that, he can build an Ace from an auxiliary. There, he is blocked as he needs a Two; but he is now allowed to deal from the stock, filling auxiliary spaces before dealing to the waste pile.

Let's say he deals the 2H, K C, as auxiliaries and the 8C to the waste pile. The King must remain in the tableau, where it becomes a dead card. But he can build the Two on the foundation, as it is double the Ace showing there. From the auxiliaries, he builds the Four on the Two and the Eight on the Four. Twice eight is sixteen; deducting thirteen leaves three, so he builds the Three on the Eight.

On the Three he builds the Six; on the Six, he builds the Queen, which stands for twelve. Twice twelve is twenty-four, and deducting thirteen leaves eleven, so a Jack is now needed. Since there is none available, more cards are dealt to fill auxiliary spaces and the waste pile, so play can continue. When building is blocked, the player just keeps dealing into the waste pile until he gets a card needed.

Kings can be moved from the waste pile to auxiliary spaces, but that is not wise at the start, because the player is allowed to deal through the pack three times. Therefore, it may be better to let the Kings stay in the waste pile until the final round. The second and third deals are made in the regular way, by turning down the waste pile and dealing from the top of the new stock.

The game is won if all cards are built on the single foundation with the exception of the Kings, which will then either be occupying spaces in the tableau or will form all that is left of the waste pile. They may then be added to the foundation to certify the win.

For convenience, a list of cards is given below, with their doubled values, showing the builds.

ACE $(1 + 1 = 2)$	**calls for a TWO**
TWO $(2 + 2 = 4)$	**calls for a FOUR**
THREE $(3 + 3 = 6)$	**calls for a SIX**
FOUR $(4 + 4 = 8)$	**calls for an EIGHT**
FIVE $(5 + 5 = 10)$	**calls for a TEN**
SIX $(6 + 6 = 12)$	**calls for a QUEEN**
SEVEN $(7 + 7 = 14 - 13 = 1)$	**calls for an ACE**
EIGHT $(8 + 8 = 16 - 13 = 3)$	**calls for a THREE**
NINE $(9 + 9 = 18 - 13 = 5)$	**calls for a FIVE**
TEN $(10 + 10 = 20 - 13 = 7)$	**calls for a SEVEN**
JACK $(11 + 11 = 22 - 13 = 9)$	**calls for a NINE**
QUEEN $(12 + 12 = 24 - 13 = 11)$	**calls for a JACK**

Letter "H" Solitaire

Two Packs

The tableau for this game is quite simple, so are the rules and that makes the game itself seem simple. But be wary and beware or it may trap you!

DIAGRAM "A"

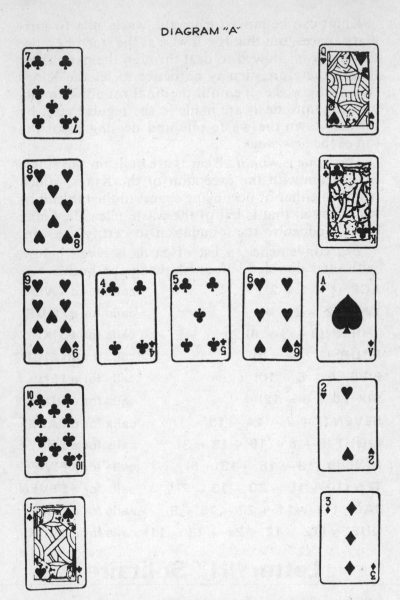

Thirteen cards are taken from the double pack, each of a different value, as suits matter not. These thirteen are used to form a letter "H" with the 7, 8, 9, 10, J forming the left side of the H, the Q, K, A,

2, 3, forming the right side, and the 4, 5, 6 forming the cross-bar.

This is shown in the upper portion of the illustrated tableau. (Diagram A) Allowance is made for two waste piles, as indicated. The player deals from the face down stock, turning up cards and building them on the tableau in ascending sequence, all cards forming the letter H are foundations, and since there is no following suit, building is easy at first, as there are thirteen values on which cards may be placed.

These chances decrease as the building continues and values begin to duplicate themselves. There are eight cards in each sequence, the purpose being to terminate the builds so they run 7, 8, 9, 10, J, Q, K, A; 8, 9, 10, J, Q, K, A, 2; and so on. At the finish, the left side of the H will therefore be formed by packets showing A, 2, 3, 4, 5, on the left side, 6, 7, 8, 9, 10 down the right side, and J, Q, K across the bar. This is shown in the lower illustration. (Diagram B)

Careful check must be kept on this, or the player may build beyond the proper limit for a foundation pile. If he notices this soon enough, he can correct it, otherwise the game must be abandoned. It is a good plan to turn down each pile after it has been completed, so there can be no mistake from then on.

As stated, the first builds are easy, but the player runs into blocks as he proceeds. Whenever he can not build, he places the dealt card face up in a waste pile, of which there are two, as already mentioned. This is where good judgement enters. If all go in one pile, they will block each other, but by choosing between them, the player may place cards where they will be handy when needed. Always, the top card of each waste pile can be built on one of the foundations, so the player should watch for such opportunities.

Cards can not be transferred from one foundation to another; nor can they be transferred between waste piles. There are no transfers whatever in this

DIAGRAM "B"

game. It is a matter of straight builds from stock to foundations. Otherwise, the cards go on to the waste piles, but are still available there. Only one deal through the double pack is allowed.

Lady of the House

Two Packs

The tableau for this game is elaborate, but the play itself is simple and direct, with good judgement figuring in it. From the double pack, the eight Aces are arranged face up in two rows. Order does not matter, as builds on these foundations are made according to values only, Ace up to King, with no regard for suits.

The double pack is then thoroughly shuffled and from it are dealt four heaps of twelve cards each. These are dealt face down; then each pile is turned face up, and the four piles are set in a row above the Aces. These become auxiliary piles with their top cards available for play.

Now comes an unusual preliminary feature. The remainder of the pack is sorted into values: Twos, Threes, Fours, right on up to Kings. These are arranged in separate packets of one to four cards, which are placed face up in a semicircle above the auxiliary piles. These serve as reserve packets.

If any values are missing — like Jacks — that space is left open in the semicircle. This means that all cards of that value must be buried somewhere in the auxiliary piles.

The illustrated tableau shows the entire arrangement. The uppermost cards of the auxiliary piles consist of a Four, Ten, Nine and Queen. Special note is made of this before play begins. Since the whole pack is included in the Tableau, there is no stock nor any waste pile in this game.

As stated, cards are built on the foundation Aces,

in ascending sequence of values only. Builds are
made from the auxiliary piles whenever possible, in
order to bring new auxiliary cards into play and
get rid of the auxiliary piles entirely. When such
builds are impossible, the player builds from the reserve piles.

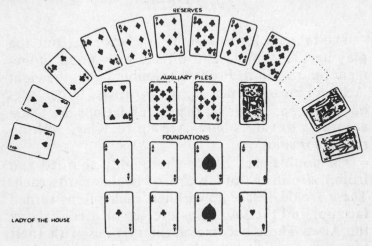

In the illustrated tableau, he would have to build
a Two and Three from the reserves in order to reach
the Four on an auxiliary pile. He could then continue with a Five, Six, Seven and Eight from the reserves, giving him a chance to play a Nine and a Ten
from the auxiliaries. Since there are no Jacks among
the reserves, the player can not build higher to get
at the Queen that shows on an auxiliary pile.

Of course, if a Jack should be uncovered on one
of the auxiliary piles, the player would immediately
build it, and then use the Queen. If a Two should be
uncovered, he would build it on an Ace. If not, he
goes back to the reserves, building from them until
he can build from an auxiliary pile.

A player is not forced to build from the reserves,
and he should avoid it if he can. Take a case where
he adds a Nine from an auxiliary pile, but has nothing higher among the auxiliaries. It would be no use

to build Ten, Jack, Queen, King from the reserves, if
they were showing there, because those can be added
any time. He would build with lower cards from the
reserves in order to build from the auxiliaries. Then,
higher values might appear on the auxiliary piles,
so they could be built from those instead of from the
reserves.

Some players go by the rule that when there is a
space among the reserve packets at the start of the
game, it can be filled from an auxiliary pile, at the
first chance. In the illustrated tableau, that would
apply to the Jack packet. If the player wants to build
the first Jack that comes along, he can fill the reserve space with the next Jack. But that is allowed
only with an original space. After that, no cards can
be moved from auxiliary piles to the reserves.

The game can be made easier, if wanted, by allowing fills from auxiliaries to reserves; but only when
there is a space and the game is blocked unless such
a move is made. That is up to the individual player.

Kings and Aces

Two Packs

The Kings and Aces are taken from a double pack
to form a simple tableau, with the eight Kings in
two columns at the left and the eight Aces in two
columns at the right. These, with a waste pile which
is dealt later, compose the whole tableau.

The remainder of the double pack is thoroughly
shuffled. From that stock, cards are dealt face up
and built on the Aces in ascending sequences, according to suits, the Two of Diamonds going on an
Ace of Diamonds, a Three of Diamonds on the Two,
on up to the King of Diamonds.

WINDMILL

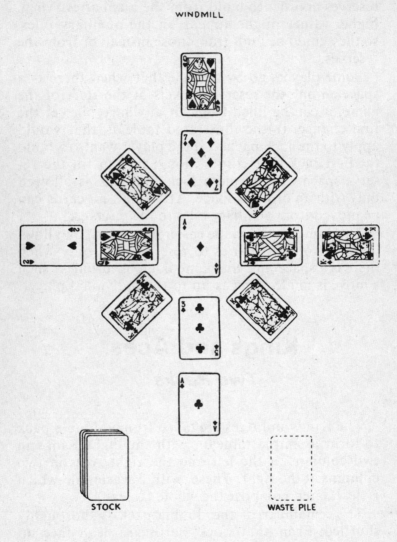

STOCK   WASTE PILE

The game is won when all the Kings are finally dealt on to the foundation. Some players make the game harder by using only Kings in the tableau, dealing Aces as foundations as they turn up from the shuffled pack. The game winds up the same, with all eight Kings on the foundations.

In any case, only one deal is made through the pack, the player winning or losing according to the way it turns out.

The Round Dance

Two Packs

This tableau takes the form of an old-fashioned dance with eight couples, represented by the Kings and Queens of a double pack. At the start, Fives and Sixes are used, making sixteen cards in all, the whole purpose being to build on these foundations according to specified rules and finish with the Kings and Queens, according to suits.

Like such dances, the game begins with a circle. The Fives and Sixes are removed from the double pack and are set in pairs, the Five to the left, the Six to the right, as you proceed around the circle. Colors should be alternated and for full convenience, the suits should run in regular order, as Spades, Hearts, Clubs, Diamonds, twice around.

The illustrated tableau shows such an arrangement with provision being made for a waste pile that goes in the exact center of the tableau. From the face down stock, the player deals cards into this central pile, turning each face up as he does so. He watches for cards that can be built on the foundations and uses them for that purpose as fast as they appear.

Builds are made in descending sequence on each

Five, in the order 5, 4, 3, 2, A, K, all of the same suit. When the King is reached, that foundation is complete. The builds are in ascending sequence on each Six, in the order 6, 7, 8, 9, 10, J, Q, all of the same suit, ending with the Queen.

ROUND DANCE

If this is accomplished, the royal couples will all be in their places, ready for the dance. Always, the top card of the waste pile is available for play, so there are times when cards that have been buried there may be reclaimed by gradually playing off those that have been dealt on it. Thanks to the double pack, there is more chance of this than if only one pack happened to be in the game.

That is all there is to the "Round Dance" but the fact that the rules are so simple makes the game speedy and easy to play. After dealing through the entire double pack, the player is allowed to turn the waste pile face down and start dealing from it as a new stock, again forming a waste pile.

Twice through is the limit. The pack must be built to Kings and Queens by the end of the second deal, or the game is lost.

The Big Wheel
Two Packs

The original tableau is formed with twelve cards which are dealt in four rows of three cards each, squarely in the center of the table. That allows room around the edges for twenty-four packets of four cards each, which are to be added to the tableau in course of play. Those form the big wheel which gives the game its name.

Aces are either discarded before the game begins, or are weeded out and laid aside as play proceeds. This is one game of solitaire that is unusual in that Aces are eliminated, although in most solitaires, they play an important part. With no Aces, there are no foundations, nor any building in the ordinary sense.

Instead, the whole purpose is to put together three cards of different values that up to a total of exactly eighteen. Numbered cards alone are used to hit the total, but a picture card must be added to each group to make it official.

Sample groups would be $2 + 6 + 10 = 18$; $4 + 5 + 9 = 18$; $3 + 7 + 10 = 18$; and other such combinations. However, $4 + 4 + 10$; or $2 + 8 + 8$ will not do, as they contain two cards that are alike.

Care must be taken almost from the start, or certain cards may be exhausted toward the finish. A player may find himself stuck with impossible com-

binations like 9 + 9 or 6 + 5 + 4 + 3, both of which
total 18, but will not do, because the rule specifies
just *three cards* of *different values.* Plus a picture card!

BIG WHEEL

The illustrated tableau shows the original twelve
cards with dotted spaces where the groups are to go.
From those, a Two, Six and Ten can be placed with
a Jack, making an eighteen group; so can a Six,
Seven and Five, with a King. But the Three, Five
and Nine won't do, because there is no available
picture card to complete that group.

However, as fast as cards are formed into groups,
the player deals new cards from the remainder of the
pack to fill the spaces among the original twelve. So
if a picture card is dealt, it could be added to Three,
Five and Nine, to make a four-card group that could
be placed on the rim of the big wheel.

If the game is blocked, so that none of the twelve cards can be grouped according to the rules, a new set of twelve cards is dealt upon those now in the center of the tableau. Play resumes after the deal and new groups are formed, if possible. As cards are uncovered, they can be included, for any card that shows is usable in making a total of eighteen.

But the player is no longer allowed to fill spaces as he goes along. He forms all the groups he can; then deals another set of twelve cards upon the center tableau, filling spaces while covering the cards that still show. This continues until the whole pack has been dealt. If the player can clear the board and complete the big wheel, he wins. If not, he loses.

Once cards are covered, the game naturally becomes more difficult, but if good judgement is used in choosing the top cards, others suitable for future groups can be brought to light.

Clover Leaves

Two Packs

The entire pack is used for the tableau, the four Aces being placed in a row as foundations and the rest of the cards forming overlapping groups of three cards each. There are eighteen of these and they resemble clover leaves, which is how the game gets its name.

All the clover leaves are regarded as auxiliary heaps. They are simply dealt at random at the start, the Aces being removed as foundations during the deal. The front card of each leaf, being free, may be built on the foundation of its suit, as 2 D on A D, and 3 D on 2 D, up to the K D. Once such a card is plucked from the clover, the next is available.

FOUNDATIONS

CLOVER LEAVES

These front cards may also be transferred from one group to another, but in doing that, it must be put on a card of the same suit, but in descending sequence. In the illustrated tableau, the 7 C can be put on the 8 C and the 6 C on the 7C, in accord with this rule. The 3 C can also be transferred to the 4 C in the same way.

Such transfers make more cards available for building and the more the merrier, as once the front card is built, the rest follow in rotation. The main task, however, is to get to the bottom card of each leaf, rather than have it remain blocked and unplayable.

When all cards of a clover leaf have been built or transferred, the empty space must remain in that condition, as there is no filling in this game. After play is blocked, the remaining clovers are gathered, shuffled, and dealt to form new groups of three cards each. If one clover happens to be a leaf or two short, it does not matter.

The game continues as before, and if blocked again, the left over clovers can be gathered, shuffled and given a third deal, which is the last. If the player manages to build all foundations up to Kings, he wins; if not, he loses.

There is one helpful rule that may be applied just after a third deal is made. If the King of any suit is above another card of that same suit, the player is allowed to bring the other card above the King. An example of this would be K S on 10 D on 9 S. The 9 S would be brought to the top to make the clover 9 S on K S on 10 D.

Unless this is done, the King will block the building of its suit, making it useless to continue the game. An odd card of another suit — like the 10 D — does not matter, because if the player builds up to the King, that card will be available for play and possibly be the opener directed toward victory.

The Scarecrow

Two Packs

The tableau requires 30 cards, dealt from a double pack.

Below, a card is turned up as a foundation. Whatever its value — say a Five — that establishes the remaining foundations, eight in all. The purpose is to build from such foundations in ascending sequence, in this case, 5, 6, 7, 8, 9, 10, J, Q, K, A, 2, 3, 4. Suits do not matter; each sequence is built according to values only. Finally, a card is turned up from the stock to start a waste pile.

The play is very simple. Cards are taken from among the auxiliaries to start foundations and build up from them. When no more cards are available among the auxiliaries, they are taken from the extras, if available there. Any spaces among the auxiliaries are not filled; but any that occur among the extras are filled from the waste pile or by dealing from the stock.

Whenever possible, go back to the auxiliaries for builders, as they always take precedence. The extras come next in order. The number of auxiliaries decreases as the game proceeds, until often, all may be gone. That throws a heavier burden on the extras and when none of them can be built, cards are dealt from the stock into the waste pile until a playable card appears there.

Sometimes two or more such cards are needed to break the block. But once it is broken, the player must go back to building from the auxiliaries if he can; if not, he builds from the reserves, which are replaced immediately from the stock or waste pile.

In the illustrated tableau, the foundation card is the 5 H. So the 5 C, 5 S, 5 D are taken from the auxiliaries and placed beside the 5 H as new foundations. The 6 S and 7 H are built on one Five; the 6 D and 7 S on another. That uses all cards that are immediately available among the auxiliaries.

Builds can then be made from the extras, representing the figure's arms. The only possible build is the 8 H which can go on either the 7 H or 7 S. It is immediately replaced from the stock or waste pile. Assume that the 9 C is dealt from the stock. As a new reserve card, the 9 C is built immediately on the 8 H.

The player then reverts to the auxiliaries, as they take precedence. From them, he can build 9, 10, J, Q, K, A in sequence. From the extras, he would build the 2 C, then revert to the auxiliaries again, finishing the build with the 3 S and 4 D. That would leave two spaces among the extras, to be filled by dealing two more cards from the stock.

When builds are temporarily blocked, cards are dealt from the stock on to the waste pile. Builds are allowed from the waste pile whenever it is impossible to build from the auxiliaries or the extras. But as soon as spaces occur among the extras, they must be filled.

Sometimes a player can work back through the waste pile, unloading its cards by filling spaces among the extras, thereby leading to new builds. When the entire pack is finely dealt, the waste pile is turned over to form a new stock, which is dealt through a second time. To win, the player must build out all foundations by the end of the second deal.

Despite its complex appearance and its special rules, this game is very simple as it is strictly a question of building on foundations.

The Fish Bone

Two Packs

The tableau in this game is formed during the course of play and is ornamental as well as useful. The ornamental part is provided by the Kings and Queens, which have no active application in the game, but add to the fun.

The double pack is shuffled and cards are dealt in three rows of two cards each, but only cards with numerical values, Ace up to Ten. If any picture appear in the deal, they are treated in the following way:

The Jacks are dealt to form a long column of eight separate cards. Since they are placed as they appear in the deal, it is a good plan to allow gaps in the column. so the Jacks will finally wind up in alternating order, as Hearts. Diamonds, Clubs. Spades, Hearts, Diamonds, Clubs, Spades, which makes it

GRIDDLE
[AUXILIARIES]

STOCK   WASTE

FOUNDATIONS

easy to keep track of them in later play.

As the Kings and Queens appear, they are placed alongside their respective Jacks as shown in the tableau, being set at an angle, to provide the appearance of a fish bone, which is the ornamental part.

The Jacks are the foundations in this game, but all the building is in downward sequence, running J, 10, 9, 8, 7, 6, 5, 4, 3, 2, A, terminating with the Aces as Kings and Queens are not considered. Each of these descending sequences must consist of cards of the same suit as the Jack that forms the foundation.

After the six auxiliary cards have been dealt as described, plus any Jacks, Queens and Kings that appear, the player may start building on the Jacks from the griddle, as the six auxiliaries are called. This building is done in descending sequence. The player may also build one auxiliary card upon another, but in ascending sequence.

This was not allowable in older versions of the game, but is generally acceptable today. However, these transfers among the griddle cards raise an important point; namely, whether they should be done singly, or in packets, once the latter have been formed. Since building by units would require duplicates, it is preferable to build by packets when the game reaches that stage.

In the tableau illustrated, all picture cards are shown in place to give an idea of the tableau's eventual appearance. But it can be assumed that only one J D and one J S have appeared by the time the six original auxiliaries have been dealt. At the point shown, the player can build the 10D on the J D, and also put the 5S on the 4S and the 8H on the 7H in the griddle.

That leaves three spaces in the griddle. These are filled by dealing from the stock, the remaining portion of the double pack. In dealing from the stock, the player may also build directly on the Jacks, in descending sequence; and on the griddle, in ascending sequence, whenever has a chance to do so. In filling spaces in the griddle, transfers of auxiliary cards become possible as mentioned earlier.

As examples, if the player should deal a 3S, 9H, 10 H to fill the griddle spaces. He would put the packet containing the 4S and 5S on the 3S. He would put the 9H on the 8H and the 10H on the 9H, since no J H is yet in the foundation column. Again, there would be three spaces in the griddle to be filled from the stock and followed by any build or moves that might be made.

As soon as a J H is dealt, it would go in the foundation column and the 10H, 9H, 7H could be built on it from their griddle pile, in reverse sequence to their own. That would leave another space to fill from the stock, as spaces can not be filled by moving cards from griddle piles themselves, as they must be moved intact.

When play from the stock is blocked, further cards are dealt into a face up waste pile, enabling the deal to continue. If the top card of the waste pile becomes available, it can be used just like a card dealt from the stock. This often happens when a Jack turns up as a new foundation card.

The ornamental Kings and Queens play an actual though slight part in the game, because they can only be placed if a Jack of the corresponding suit is already in the foundation column, with an opening beside it. Unless that is the case, the King or Queen must go into the waste pile. While there, it blocks the card it covers, which might just happen to become available if uncovered. Kings or Queens may be played from the waste pile if available when their Jack appears, so they really belong in the game and should not be discarded from the pack as useless.

By the time the double pack has been dealt

through once, all eight Jacks will be in their places as foundations, though Kings and Queens that showed up early will still be in the waste pile. With the deal finished, the waste pile is turned face down to become a new but depleted stock, which is dealt through a second time, just as before.

During this deal, the player is sure to place all the remaining Kings and Queens, and his hope is that he will be able to build the rest of the foundations clear down to Aces and win the game, though that is often difficult. The game ends with this second deal.

Congress Solitaire

Two Packs

The tableau is formed by eight Aces from the double pack, laid in two cross rows, with eight other cards dealt from the shuffled pack to form two columns of four cards each, left and right. The rows are the foundations and the colunns are athe auxiliary piles. One more card is dealt face up to start a waste pile, while the rest of the pack is kept face down as a stock.

The game has the customary purpose of building each foundation from Ace up to King, using cards of the same suit in each instance. The auxiliary cards may be used for such builds. Also, auxiliary cards may be transferred from one pile to another, in either column, in descending sequence, but here, value alone matters, suits being disregarded.

In the illustrated tableau, the player would first build the auxiliary 2C on either A C. He can not build the 3D on the 2C because it is the wrong suit. But he can transfer the 3D to either the 4S or the 4D because suit does not matter. But is it better to put it on the 4D. Then if the player builds the 3D he can follow by building the 4D. In this tableau, he also transfers the 8C to the 9D, making three spaces in all.

The Q C is taken from the waste pile to fill one space. The J H is then transferred to the Q C so there are still three auxiliary spaces. Since there is now no waste pile, cards are dealt from the stock to fill the spaces and an extra card is dealt to start the waste pile again. During this, new builds or transfers may be made, if opportunities arise.

With builds made and spaces filled, the player continues to deal from the stock to the waste pile. He can make new builds from either the stock or the waste pile; and he can also add to descending sequences on auxiliary piles. Each card dealt from the stock or the uppermost card on the waste pile is always available.

So are the cards on the auxiliary piles, which should be kept slightly spread to see what lies beneath. A player might have a 7D on an 8H, with a chance to build the 8H. In that case, if another pile had an 8S on top, he could transfer the 7D to the 8S and build the 8H. But only the top card of a pile may be shifted in that way.

But there are times when a player may hold back on a build or transfer from one of the auxiliary pile, rather than form a space. This is because spaces can not be filled from the auxiliary piles. They must be filled from the waste pile when possible. So if a player doesn't like or want the top card of the waste pile, he holds back on forming spaces until he has dealt one or more cards from the stock to see what they offer. Once such cards go into the waste pile, they take precedence in filling auxiliary spaces.

Some players go by a more liberal rule, allowing spaces to be filled from the stock or the waste pile, as desired. In that case, the stock should be kept face up, so the player sees each new card as it comes along, giving him choice between the stock and the waste pile, or he can look at the top cards.

Only one deal is allowed, so the game is hard to win, but it offers many "outs" before a player is finally blocked, which is why this form of solitaire appeals to serious players.

Parliament Solitaire

This game is played very much like "Congress" but with the following modification that renders it more difficult:

Instead of laying out the eight Aces as foundations, the game may be started with only the auxiliary columns, keeping them sufficiently apart so that the Aces can be set between, whenever they appear during the deal. This makes the game somewhat harder.

Many special transfers are possible from one pile to another, to get at cards needed for immediate builds. The more the game is played, the more no-

ticeable these become, so the best way to find out is
by trying it.

The Dutch Windmill

Two Packs

This is a game with a rather elaborate tableau, but
its play is quite simple. A red Ace is placed in the
center of the tableau and the four black Kings are
then taken from the double pack and set at angles,
extending from the corners of the key ACE. Four
blades are furnished the wind mill by dealing eight
cards from the shuffled pack, face up, extending in
pairs from the ace, vertically and horizontally.

The arrangement is shown in the illustrated tableau. The Ace represents the main foundation, on
which cards are to be built in ascending sequence,
Ace to King, regardless of suit. Another Ace is then
to be built on the central pile, continuing up to
King; and this goes on with two more sets, until
the center is stacked with a pile of 48 cards.

Meanwhile, the player builds down on the four
Kings, which represent lesser foundations, running
in descending sequence, King down to Ace. In order
to keep building the central pile, it is allowable to
transfer a card from one of the corner piles, if the
chance occurs. Suits do not matter in the descending
sequences. Only values count in this game.

The eight cards composing the blades of the windmill are reserve cards, which can be built on any of
the foundations. Spaces in the blades are filled by
dealing from the stock, or using the uppermost card
of the waste pile, which is always available. Working back through the waste pile is essential to this
game, as the pack can be dealt through only once.

In transferring cards from the downward builds to
the center pile, it is not allowable to transfer the

AUXILIARIES   FOUNDATIONS

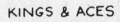

KINGS & ACES

Kings. Those black Kings remain as fixed foundations clear to the end of the game. The purpose, of course, is to complete all building during the single deal; four stacks or Aces up to red Kings in the big center foundation; four black Kings down to any Aces in the corner foundations.

Whirligig

In this form of "Dutch Windmill", only the central Ace is used as a starting foundation. The corner foundations are left vacant, but as Kings appear during the deal, they are placed in position there. In this case, any Kings do for foundations; it does not matter whether they are red or black.

That stiffens the game somewhat, but as a help to the player, he may transfer Kings from corner foundations to the center pile, if that will help in building up the center. Once a King has been so transferred, the player uses another King to form the corner foundation. Otherwise, the rules follow those of the "Dutch Windmill."

The Courtyard

Two Packs

In this tableau, twelve cards are dealt face up to form three sides of a courtyard, four to a side. The end nearest to the player is left open and the space in the center of the court is to receive the Aces as foundations. There will be eight of these, as the game is played with a double pack.

In addition, there is the usual stock, or remainder of the pack, from which cards are dealt face up to form a waste pile. The uppermost card of that pile is always available for play.

The purpose is to build the foundation Aces up to Kings, following suit on each foundation. The cards

forming the sides of the courtyard are auxiliaries
and are available for building. They can also be
transferred to form auxiliary piles, in descending sequence according to suits. Whenever a space occurs
in the sides of the courtyard, a card may be dealt
from the stock or moved from the waste pile to fill it.

Cards from stock or waste pile can be built on the
ascending foundations, or placed on the descending
sequences of the auxiliary piles, as desired. All transfers among auxiliary piles are made singly, card by
card; never in groups.

In the illustrated tableau, the auxiliaries have been
dealt to form the sides of the court and the first card

has been dealt to start the waste pile. Play would proceed:

Build the Ace of Heart as a foundation, followed by the Two from the waste pile and the Three from an auxiliary. Transfer Q S on to K S. Transfer 7S on 8S and 6S on 7S. Be careful not to transfer the Six first, as the combined Six and Seven can not be transferred to the Eight.

Spades are filled from the stock and a new card is dealt to the waste pile. Builds and transfers are then resumed if any are possible. If not, a deal is made to the waste pile.

Deuces Up

Two Packs

This game differs from "Courtyard" in one respect only: Deuces are built as foundations instead of Aces. Further cards are built in ascending sequences, according to suits, with Aces following Kings as the final cards. All other rules of "Courtyard" apply to "Deuces Up."

Some players treat these games as alternates. They begin in the usual fashion, but do not decide the form of game until the courtyard has been dealt, or until after transfers have been made and spaces filled. If Aces show up, they are used as foundations, as in "Courtyard". If Deuces turn up, instead of Aces, the player switches the game to "Deuces Up."

Lucas

Two Packs

The over-sized tableau used in this game is a help rather than a hindrance to its play. The eight Aces are first removed from the double pack and set in a row to form foundations, which are to be built in ascending sequence (Ace up to King) in accordance with suits. The pack is then shuffled and thirty-nine cards are dealt in thirteen columns of three cards each, preferably in overlapping style, all face up, forming auxiliary piles. The remainder of the pack forms a stock.

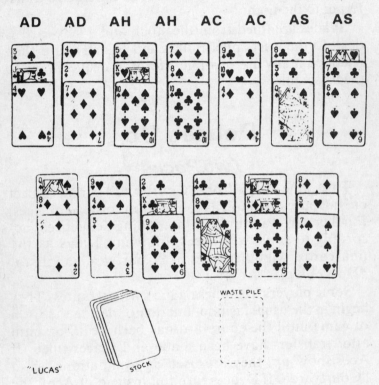

Play is simple and direct. Any card at the bottom of an auxiliary column is available, either for building in upward sequence according to suit; or for transfer to another column in downward sequence, also according to suit. When the cards of a column have all been removed, leaving a space, it can be filled with any available card. But in all transfers, cards must be moved singly; never in groups.

After a few spaces have been formed, it is possible to make transfers by degrees, or steps, in order to get at needed cards which be then may be buried in a lengthy column. Also, as foundations build higher, they often meet a descending sequence formed on an auxiliary column. The cards can then be built from the column on to the foundation in rapid succession.

When play is blocked, cards are dealt from the face down stock and either built on the foundations or placed on the auxiliary columns in descending sequence, if possible. If not, the cards from the stock go into a face up waste pile, where the uppermost card is always available. By playing back from the waste pile, it is often possible to reclaim cards that seem hopelessly buried there.

This is important, because the player can deal through the stock only once, as a second trip through often would make the game too easy.

In the illustrated tableau, the player would immediately build the Two, Three and Four of Diamonds on one of the Aces. He could then transfer the Seven of Diamonds on to the Eight (freed by the 2D) and then build the other Two of Diamonds on to the second Ace.

Other transfers among the auxiliaries would include: Six of Spades on Seven; Nine of Spades on Ten; Nine of Clubs on Ten; Queen of Clubs on freed King; Jack of Clubs on Queen; Three of Spades on Four. This would give the player a space in the first column, giving him several choices for his next move.

St. Helena

Two Packs

This game is similar to "Lucas" but is much harder to beat, as it has less columns and there are no foundations to start, the Aces being placed as they become available in the tableau or during the deal from the stock.

The player begins by dealing forty cards in ten columns for four cards each:

QH	2D	6D	7H	7S	6S	10H	3D	5H	2C
KD	JC	7H	4S	9D	3C	QH	10C	KD	5H
4S	4D	7C	AD	8H	9C	QC	KS	JD	8D
QD	5S	QS	JS	JH	AS	AH	4C	5S	JS

In the illustration, the AS and AH are set as foundations; the first JS is moved on to the QS. The AD is then set as a foundation and the 4S may be transferred to either 5H.

All these cards are dealt face up in overlapping form — as in "Lucas" — and only the bottom card of each column is available. Any Aces among such cards are immediately taken to start foundations and cards of proper suits are built on them in ascending sequences. Transfers are made among the auxiliary columns in descending sequence, by suits, as in "Lucas," and cards are later dealt from the stock into a waste pile, only one deal being allowed.

Maria Luisa

Two Packs

This game is very similar to "St. Helena" but it incorporates a modern feature that makes it more popular today. The tableau is dealt out as in "St. Helena", but there are only nine columns, instead of ten. These have four cards each, making thirty-six cards in all, and they are arranged in the usual overlapping fashion, with the cards at the foot of the columns available for play.

Available Aces are taken as foundations and built

upward in sequence to Kings, according to suits. Now comes the difference. In forming descending sequences on the auxiliary columns, cards are taken in alternating colors, as a red Eight on a black Nine, a black Seven on the red Eight, and so on.

This is like the modern game of "Canfield" with which many players are familiar, so it makes it earier for them to play. It makes the game easier, too, because there are twice as many chances in forming auxiliary columns. This is offset somewhat during the building, as the alternating colors can not be built in such rapid sequence as single suits.

Otherwise, the game is identical with "St. Helena" and goes by the same general rules.

Sultan of Turkey
Two Packs

The tableau in this unusual game is rather elaborate, but the play itself is quite simple, making it a very popular type of Solitaire. From the double pack, the eight Kings and the Aces of Hearts are removed and arranged as foundations. To the left and right are columns of four cards each, eight in all. These are reserves, but are popularly called the Divan.

The illustrated tableau shows this: The Ace of Hearts is flanked by the two Kings of Spades; the King of Hearts, in the very center, is flanked by the two Kings of Diamonds; the other King of Hearts, directly below, is flanked by the Kings of Clubs. This is a regular arrangement, but the Divan, or reserve columns, are random cards, as they happened to be dealt.

The central King of Hearts is the Sultan and remains as is. On the other Kings, or pashas, builds are made in ascending order, according to suits. Each

King is topped by an Ace, then a two and so on, up
to the Queen. The lone Ace of Hearts is treated the
same way, builds on that pile consisting of the Two,
Three and so on up to the Queen.

"SULTAN OF
TURKEY"   STOCK   PILE

Builds may be made from the Divan cards and as fast as these reserves are use, new cards from the stock are dealt to fill the spaces, but no transfers are made among the reserves. They remain as single cards until built; then the spaces are replenished as used.

When unable to build, the player deals from the stock into a face up waste pile. The top card of the waste pile is always available, either to build on foundations or to fill spaces in the Divan. In this way, the player can work back through the waste pile, sometimes reducing it quite rapidly.

After dealing through once, the waste pile is turned over and treated as a new stock. After the second deal that process is repeated. But the third deal is the last. To win, the builds must be completed by that time. The game is won when the Sultan, or central King of Hearts, is surrounded by a bevy of harem beauties, the eight Queens.

Shah of Persia

Two Packs

The simplest version of this game is very similar to "Sultan of Turkey" but less cards are used. Before the deal, all Kings are removed from the pack and eliminated from the game, except one King of Hearts, which sits in the center as the Shah. The surrounding cards, instead of being Kings, are the eight Aces, which form foundations for their respective suits.

With such a tableau to start, the game follows the rules of "Sultan of Turkey" with each suit running from Ace up to the Queen, so that the Shah, like the Sultan, is completely hemmed in by his harem if the game is won within three deals.

The Giant

Two Packs

This game is a series of tableaus, each a simple
deal of eight cards in a row. After one is played out,
the next is dealt, picking up where the last one left
off. The result is a giant spread of cards, covering
the table, since the double pack contains 104 cards.
But this can be condensed during the play.

The first row is dealt face up and any Aces are removed from it to form foundations, which are to be
built in ascending sequence according to suit. The
remainder of the row become auxiliary cards, which
can be transferred in descending sequence, in alternate colors.

Take an original deal of:

5H   AS   QD   2S   JC   9S   5C   7C

The Ace would be used to start a foundation and
the Two would be built on it, both being of the same
suit. The Jack would be transferred to the Queen,
being of the opposite color. That leaves three spaces,
which can not yet be filled. Another tableau is dealt
below the first, in the form of another row of eight
cards. This is shown in the illustrated tableaus.

The player would transfer the red Two to the
black Three; and the red Ten to the black Jack. Fill
the space with the 10C. That makes the black Nine
available for transfer to the red Ten. That leaves
another space which can be filled by the 5D, or another available card, such as the 7S, the 2H, or the
3C and 2H as a unit. Again, play is stopped.

A third tableau of eight cards is dealt as a new
row below the other two. The game goes on tableau by tableau, each new row blocking the cards
above, but sometimes offering special chances of
their own, which puts interest in the game.

Not only single cards and complete sequences can

be transferred from one auxiliary pile to another, or used to fill spaces, but the same can be done with partial sequences. This helps a lot in building. If a player needs a Seven of Diamonds, he can transfer a black Six (and any sequence below it) on a Seven of Hearts, if one is available. It is also allowable to bring back cards from the builds, if they are needed to form a descending sequence on an auxiliary pile.

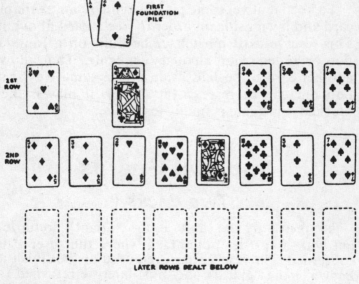

FIRST FOUNDATION PILE

1ST ROW

2ND ROW

LATER ROWS DEALT BELOW

"GIANT"

The player must always remember that each new tableau, blocks everything dealt above it, until some play has been made in the newly dealt row. If no play is possible another tableau, or row of eight, must be dealt. But once a row is "broken", play can be made with available cards above. Sometimes, in dealing a tableau, a player may luckily place a card in sequence, as by dealing a red Ten on a black Jack in the row above. That counts in his favor if he does.

The "Giant" is a hard game to win, but offers so many prospects that a player can remain hopeful clear down to the bottom line, where a careful study of the situation may make it possible to work back up through the tableau. So the game is fun, even when it is finally stopped.

To keep it alive, some players remove an available card and lay it aside, in order to free a card above it. This reserve card must later be built on a foundation or added to an auxiliary sequence. That allows another card to be laid aside in the same way, but only one can be reserved at a time. If play is then blocked, the game is finally lost.

Imperial Guards

Two Packs

This is exactly the same as the "Giant" solitarie, but with a further advantage where the reserve is concerned. The reserve card removed at the finish is known as the "guard" and must later be returned to play as already described as an added rule in the "Giant."

But the player can lay aside more than a single card to form the guard. He can take away a whole sequence or part of one, from the tableau, so that the "guard" may consist of a half a dozen cards or more. As further help, this reserve may be laid out in a row, so each and every card can be played individually when the chance comes.

However, all reserve cards of the "guard" must be built or added to auxilliary cards before the player is allowed to call the Imperial Guard again!

Shady Lanes

Two Packs

The tableau is simple, but somewhat unusual in the way it is handled. First, deal eight Aces from the double pack, four blacks face up in a row; four reds face up in a second row. The reason is that these foundations are to be built in ascending sequence to Kings, but not by suit, nor by value alone, as in most solitaires.

Instead, the sequences are to be in alternating colors: Red Two on black Ace; black Three on red Two and so on. In the second row, the order would be: Black Two on red Ace; red Three on black Two and so on. By having the rows so each contains Aces of the same color. it is easier to keep track of this.

Next deal a third row of four face up cards, as a further portion of the tableau. These cards are dealt at random from the shuffled double pack and they represent the beginning of Auxiliary Piles. Below that, deal a fourth row of face up cards at random. This becomes the Reserve Row, and consists of single cards only. The remainder of the pack is the stock, and from it one card is dealt face up to start a waste pile.

Play is simple, but must be noted carefully to avoid mistakes that might spoil the game. The Auxiliary cards can be built on the foundations, as described. Auxiliaries can also be transferred to others in the same row, in descending sequence of alternate colors. Cards from the Reserve can be put on Auxil-

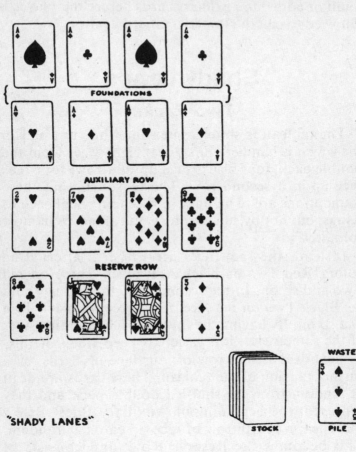

iary Piles in the same descending sequence. Whenever there is a space in the Auxiliary Row, it is immediately filled by a card from the Reserve Row, which is moved up for that purpose.

Vacancies in the reserve row are immediately filled from the waste pile, or from the stock, if all cards in the waste pile have been used. But the reserves can not be built on the foundations, nor transferred among themselves. They are as stated, strictly reserves, which are used as aids to increase or fill the auxiliary piles.

Cards that turn up in the waste pile can be built on the foundations. They can also be added to descending sequences in the auxiliary piles. The top card of the waste pile is always available for such play, as are cards dealt from the stock, which would otherwise go on the waste pile. But none of those can be used to fill spaces in the Auxiliary row. Those spaces can only be filled from the reserve.

There are times when a card from the waste pile may be used to fill a space in the reserve, and the player may be able to fill a space in the auxiliary row with that same card, and even build it on a foundation, all in one continuous move. But it is really a series of regular steps, not just a single action; and this must be remembered.

The illustrated tableau gives an example of this. The red Two can be built on a black Ace, and the black Nine transferred to the red Ten, leaving two spaces among the Auxiliary Piles. One of these would be filled by the black Queen from the reserves; while the red Jack could then be taken from the reserve Row and placed in descending sequence on the black Queen.

Since that leaves two spaces in the Reserve Row, the black Three could be taken from the waste pile to fill one of those spaces. From there, it would be used to fill the space in the Auxiliary Row. From there, it would be built on the red Two in the foundation rows.

Cards from the stock would then be dealt to fill spaces in the Reserve Row, which in turn could be used to fill the space among the Auxiliary Piles. When blocked, cards are dealt from the stock into the waste pile in hope of playing them out later and eventually completing all eight foundations. This must be done in one deal through the stock.

Once a player begins to unload from the auxiliary piles on the foundations, this game can move very rapidly, due to the alternating colors, which is why many players like it.

The Twilight Zone

Two Packs

This is a restricted version of "Shady Lanes" which is a harder game, because close attention must be given to established procedure. No cards from the waste pile can be built upon foundations or placed in descending sequence on the auxiliary piles. Waste pile cards can only be used to fill spaces in the Reserve Row, which becomes a vital "zone" in the game.

Cards dealt from the stock can be built on foundations or placed in descending sequence on Auxiliary Piles, but once in the waste pile they are dead. until an opening occurs in that in-between zone. Always, a space in the auxiliary row must be filled from the reserve zone ahead of any other play. Also, a space in the reserve zone must be filled immediately from the waste pile, whether the player wants that card or not.

Often, desirable cards will go to waste, but as compensation the player is allowed to deal through the pack a second time, turning over the waste-pile to form a new stock. Sharp building or filling spaces from reserve zone into the auxiliary row also will help the player's cause.

The Four Winds

The unusual tableau in this game consists of four Aces, as foundations, representing the Four Winds. They are placed well apart at the points of the compass, North, East, South and West. The pack is then shuffled and four cards are dealt face up, beside each Ace. These become Reserve Squares. The remainder of the pack is the stock, from which a card is dealt face up to start a waste pile.

The purpose is to build the foundations up to Kings, using cards of the same suit. These may be taken from the reserve squares or the waste pile, where the uppermost card is always available, Cards dealt from the stock may also be built directly on to the foundations. Whenever a space occurs in a reserve square, it may be filled, but only with a card of the same suit as the Ace governing that square. Such fills can be made from other squares, or from either the stock or waste pile.

The illustrated tableau shows how simply this works. On the A C, the player builds the 2C and 3C. On the A S, he builds the 2S. That leaves a space in the Diamond Square (vacated by the 2C) which can be filled with any Diamond. It leaves two spaces in the Heart Square (vacated by the 3C and 2S) which can be filled by any Hearts.

There are available cards in the other squares as well as one in the waste pile, but it may be better to deal a few cards from the stock before making such moves, in order to see what may turn up. Sometimes neat shifts can be made between squares, such as moving a Heart from the Diamond square to the Heart square, so that a Diamond can be moved from the waste pile into the Diamond square. All that can help in future builds.

It must be remembered that the squares contain reserve cards only. They can not be arranged in piles but must continually be treated as single cards. That is another reason why it is sometimes unwise to overload a reserve square with cards of its own suit. Once there, those cards can not be moved again. The only way to dispose of them is to build them.

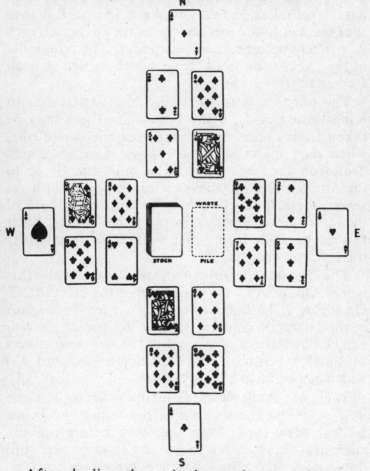

After dealing through the pack once, the waste pile is turned over and dealt through as a new stock. The game must be won in this deal, as no third deal is allowed. Always, it is possible to work back through the waste pile, furnishing fillers for the squares, or making direct builds.

Choose Your Squares

This game is an interesting variation of "Four Winds." Instead of starting with the Aces as foundations, the player simply deals four reserve squares of four cards each. If Aces appear among the squares, he uses them as foundations; if not, he deals from stock to waste pile until an Ace turns up.

During this process, he is allowed to choose his squares according to whatever suit he wants. Assuming the Ace of Hearts is his first Ace, he looks over the squares and builds the Ace beside the square he prefers as the Heart Square.

He can choose other squares even before an Ace appears, so as to shift cards into them and have them available when an Ace does appear. Such shifts may also help to prepare other squares for later play. Except for this opening feature, "Choose Your Squares" is played the same as "Four Winds."

Boxing The Compass
Two Packs

This tableau is almost identical with the single pack game of the "Four Winds", but there are two Aces (of the same suit) accompanying each corner square, and the player can build on either one.

The rules of "Four Winds" are followed throughout, including the gathering of suits in their respective corner squares, which are composed of four cards each, as in "Four Winds". But because of the double pack, the player has this special privilege:

After a corner square is filled with cards of its own suits, the player endeavors to clear it by building those cards on foundations. If he does that, he can deal or move four new cards of any suits into that square, giving him a fresh start where it is concerned.

Allowance should be made for this. If a Spade Square already contains a 10S, it might be unwise to deal or move another 10S there, as it would then be harder to clear the square by "building out."

In "Boxing the Compass", two deals are allowed through the double pack, just as in the single pack game of "Four Winds."

"Boxing The Compass"
(Sample Layout)

			AS	AS			
			3H	10S			
			6S	8H			
AD	4S	2S			9C	JH	AH
AD	KD	2H			KC	10S	AH
			3S	5D			
			KD	7D			
			AD	AC			

The 2, 3, 4 of Spades can be built on one Ace.

The 2, 3 of Hearts can be built on another.

But it would be unwise to move the 10S from the Heart Square into the Spade Square; or the K D from the Club Square into the Diamond Square, as they would duplicate cards already there, and make it harder to clear those squares.

Fourteens

The tableau consists of ten cards dealt face up, either in two vertical columns or two cross rows of five cards each. Only values are considered — not suits — and the game is simply to pair up cards that total 14.

This is similar to other "matching" games, but this one goes into higher brackets. Ace counts 1, other cards according to their number, with picture cards running Jack, 11; Queen 12; and King, 13.

In the illustrated tableau (shown below) there are two "fourteens", namely: Jack and Three (11 + 3 = 14) and Nine and Five (9 + 5 = 14).

4	7	Ace	3	9
Jack	5	4	Queen	6

When pairs have been removed, fresh cards are dealt from the stock to fill the spaces.

Fourteen combinations run: King-Ace; Queen-Two; Jack-Three; Ten-Four; Nine-Five; Eight-Six; Seven-Seven. If a pack contains two Jokers, they should be used and counted as Sevens, making three matching pairs of Sevens instead of only two.

The Double Fan
Two Packs

This tableau is twice as large as "Clover Leaves" — which is played with a single pack — because it uses a double pack. Trios of cards are laid out exactly as in "Clover Leaves" and the eight Aces are placed in a double row as foundations.

Excluding the Aces, there are 96 cards, followed throughout, the only difference being the size of the tableau and the duration of the game.

The duplication of cards often offers additional advantages in this double pack game, which is why many players prefer it to the single pack.

Elevens

This is a reversal of "Eleven O'clock", with the

purpose being to eliminate cards totalling eleven, as
they come along. Rather than make the game too
easy, the tableau is reduced to nine cards, formed in
a square of three rows each, as:

Five	Jack	Nine
Two	Ace	Two
Seven	Three	Ace

The Nine and a Two are removed, as they total
eleven. So is the Jack because all picture cards count
eleven each. That leaves three spaces in which new
cards are dealt from the stock. Any further elevens
are removed (as Ten-Ace, Six-Five, Eight-Three,
Seven-Four) as are any picture cards.

If the board is cleared, the game is won. Usually,
it is easily done.

Can-Can

The tableau in this game is dealt like the start of
Canfield, but from both ends, which is why it is called "Can-Can." The overlapping columns run 1, 2,
3, 4, 5, 6, 7 in number, as with Canfield, but from
there the deal keeps on in decreasing ratio, 6, 5, 4,
3, 2, 1.

The bottom card of each column is turned face
up, as in Canfield, but since there are only three
cards left over, they are turned face up as a reserve,
instead of remaining in a face down stock.

The tableau appears as shown below, with face
down cards (★) and face up cards (+) as indicated:

```
    +  ★  ★  ★  ★  ★  ★  ★  ★  ★  ★  +
       +  ★  ★  ★  ★  ★  ★  ★  ★  ★  +
          +  ★  ★  ★  ★  ★  ★  ★  +
             +  ★  ★  ★  ★  ★  +
                +  ★  ★  ★  +
                   +  ★  +
                      +
             +  +  +
```

Play is exactly as in Canfield, but without dealing through the pack. Instead, the three reserve cards are always available and are played as desired.

Aces are removed and used as Foundations, whenever turned up, and cards are built on them in ascending sequences by suits. Cards are transferred among auxiliary piles to form descending sequences in alternating colors. Once groups are formed, they must be moved intact; and only Kings can fill spaces.

As will be seen, this is a double-ended tableau and with so many auxiliary piles (13 in all) there are generally good chances for transfers in the early stages. This makes the game more interesting as it proceeds, with transfers figuring very heavily. But it is not always as easy as it looks, as it can become a real sticker at the finish.

Trusty Twelve

The tableau consists of twelve cards, dealt in three rows of four cards each. These are the beginnings of auxiliary piles; there are no foundations and no waste pile. The remainder of the pack, or stock, is used to fill spaces as they occur.

Cards are considered according to value only, as suits do not matter. The tableau might therefore be:

Jack	Queen	Two
Four	Eight	Four
Nine	Three	Six
Jack	Ace	Eight

Cards are transferred among the auxiliaries to form descending sequences. But once a pile has been formed, it can not be moved. Only single cards, or the card showing on the face of a pile is transferable.

The object of the game is to use up the entire pack

by forming descending sequences. Every time there is a space in the tableau, a card may be dealt from the stock to fill it. In that way, the pack is gradually diminished. But when it becomes impossible to continue forming descending sequences in the tableau, play is blocked and the game is lost.

In the tableau illustrated, a Jack can be put on the Queen to start. But a card should be dealt to fill the space before putting an Eight on the Nine. If the dealt card is a Ten, it can go on Jack, followed by by the Nine and Eight.

A Seven, if dealt, would allow a descending sequence, Nine, Eight, Seven, Six; while a Five would make it possible to form a sequence, Five, Four, Three, Two, Ace, as the Ace is always low in this game. Some chances have to be sacrificed, but the fewer the better, or the player will run short on piles as the game proceeds.

Knotty Nines

This is similar to "Trusty Twelve" but the tableau is limited to nine cards, forming a three-by-three square. The game in this form is much harder and will be lost if the player gets off to a bad start, the rules being exactly the same as in "Trusty Twelve."

Players who like a game with a hard challenge will prefer "Knotty Nines" as it can be played rapidly and started over again, whenever it goes bust. The result is that when the player does win, he gets good satisfaction from having licked something really tough.

Most players grant themselves one special privilege in this game. They turn up the top card of the stock before making transfers in the tableau. Sometimes that card can be put directly on an auxiliary pile, thus helping with another transfer.

Hidden Cards

In this fast game, the tableau uses the entire pack. Thirteen piles are dealt, consisting of four cards each. These are turned face down and numbered in rotation: 1, 2, 3, 4, up to 12, the thirteenth packet being laid aside as it contains the travelers.

The top card is taken from the Travel Pile, turned face up and inserted beneath the pile of that number. The top card of that packet is then turned up and used as a traveler.

This continues on until the game is won or lost, a new travel card being taken from the top of its packet whenever play is blocked. The fact that each travel card must be drawn "blind" makes the game a little more difficult.

All Fours

This game resembles "Travelers", but in it, Kings rate like other cards and have their own pile, Number 13. The cards are dealt accordingly and there is no "travel pile" nor any "travel cards" in the full sense of the term.

For convenience, the packets, which consist of four face down cards, should be dealt in rows of five, five, and three, so the bottom row can be regarded as Jack, Queen and King, without calculation:

1	2	3	4	5
6	7	8	9	10
J	Q	K		

Instead of a travel card, the top card of Pile 1 — the Ace pile — is turned up. Whatever its value, it is inserted beneath the proper pile and the top card of that pile is turned up and treated accordingly. This is exactly as in the game of "Hidden Cards." The purpose is to get back to the Ace pile at the very end of the game, so that all piles will contain cards entirely of their own value.

If the player gets back to the Ace pile too soon, he still has another chance. He may move along to the next pile that still has a face down card and turn that card up. He then inserts it under the pile of its number and continues as before. He wins, if he turns up all the piles.

This time, if the player is stopped, the game is over, but he can still turn up any face down cards remaining on other piles, to see if they belong there. If they do, the game is regarded as a win.

Double Canfield
Two Packs

This is the greatest of all two-pack Solitaires, but it is not played by a single player. Instead, it is played by two persons, each with a single pack.

The players are seated opposite and each deals himself a regular tableau as used in Canfield. They then play through the tableau according to the usual rules, but with this added privilege: Each is allowed to build on the other player's foundations.

This is done by consultation, so when one player's game is blocked, the other may be able to pull him out of his difficulty. Often, the favor may be returned, so whenever the game is carried through to a complete finish, it becomes a double triumph.

Saratoga

This game is similar to Canfield, but with one important difference. All the cards in the original tableau are dealt face up, allowing the player to see

those that will be coming up. That way, he can soon
tell if the game is hopeless blocked.

It also enables the player to choose between two
moves, as he can tell which is better. This eliminates
the guess work found in Canfield, giving the player
more chance of winning in Saratoga.

A special rule also works in the player's favor. If
two cards in an auxiliary pile happen to be dealt in
proper sequence, as a black Seven on a red Eight,
the player can treat them that way when he comes to
them, giving him that much more advantage. But
he does not have to consider them in sequence.

Otherwise, the rules are exactly the same as in
Canfield, but the player must be careful in moving
groups from one auxiliary pile to another as so
many face up cards may cause confusion.

San Juan Hill

Two Packs

This game is played exactly like St. Helena, but
the eight Aces are taken from the pack and placed as
foundations before he 40-card tableau is dealt. The
game became popular after the Spanish-American
War, when Teddy Roosevelt led the charge up San
Juan Hill. The eight Aces represent the hill and the
forty cards below are Teddy's Rough Riders who
made the charge. As with St. Helena, when a space
occurs, it may be filled with any available card.

Big Forty

Deal forty cards in ten overlapping columns of ten
cards each. All are face up, with the bottom card of

each column available for transfer to another, in descending value of the same suit. Aces are placed as foundations during the course of play and are built up to Kings of their suit. A stock of twelve cards is dealt into a waste pile.

Because only a single pack is used, the player can transfer groups when they become available, as putting the 10H, 9H, 8H, on the JH. Such groups can also be put in spaces. Also, the player may deal through the waste pile as often as he pleases to get at any cards he needs.

Ali Baba

Identical with *Big Forty*, but the four Aces are first set out as foundations. Forty cards are then dealt to form the tableau, with only eight as a reserve. The forty cards represent Ali Baba's band of forty thieves and the player is Ali Baba.

Assembled Aces

Procedure in this Solitaire is simple, but must be followed carefully. The pack is shuffled and cards are dealt singly into four heaps, each face down:

1   2   3   4

The last heap dealt (in this case, Number 4) is turned face up and cards are tossed away one by one until an Ace appears. This heap is laid face up, with the Ace showing. This is done with the three remaining heaps, each being placed face up on the one before it. If no Ace appears in a heap, that heap is completely discarded.

The stock is now turned face down, and cards are dealt singly into three heaps. Beginning with the heap on which the deal ends, the three heaps are tuned face up and treated as before, eliminating cards until an Ace appears. The stock is turned face down, two heaps are dealt and treated the same way. Finally a single heap is dealt and turned face up. If the Aces all have come together, the game is won.

Royal Flush

Similar to *Assembled* Aces, this Solitaire starts with a deal of five heaps, card by card:

1   2   3   4   5

The deal will end on Heap Number 2, so it is the first to be turned face up. The player then runs through the cards until he comes to an Ace, King, Queen, Jack, or Ten of any suit. He discards up to that point, then stops and keeps the "honor card" with all that follow it.

This honor card — such as the JD — establishes the suit in which the player hopes to gain a Royal Flush (A-K-Q-J-10). He goes through the other heaps, stopping whenever he comes to such a card, and adds it (with the remaining cards) to the heap before. If no honor card appears in a heap, the whole heap is discarded.

The stock is turned face down, and four heaps are dealt singly, repeating the process. Then, three heaps are dealt face down, then two, and finally one. The player wins if all cards of the Royal Flush (in this case AD, KD, QD, JD, 10D) come out together. It does not matter in what order they appear, as long as they form a group.

Thirty-Nine Steps

Two Packs

Form a tableau of thirteen columns containing three cards each, all face up, making thirty-nine cards in all, as:

**KH 3S 9C KD 4C 4H 7C JS 9C AH QH 4S QS
JS QS AD 2S JC JD 9S KC AD 10D 6H 10S 7S
8C 2H 3H KS 7D JD 5D 7H 5H 5C 10C 8H 8S**

These can be dealt in overlapping fashion, so that only lowest row of cards are available. Any such card can be moved to another column, in descending order according to suit. In this tableau, the 2H could be moved on to the 3H, so the QS could be moved on the the KS.

When blocked, a card is dealt from the face-down stock on to a waste pile, where the upper card is always available. As Aces become available, they are used to form foundations which are built upward in sequence according to suit. Only one card may be moved at a time, but when a column is cleared, any available card may be moved into the space formed thereby.

This makes it possible to work cards in and out of spaces, rearranging columns and making them longer. All this is important, as the player is not allowed to go through the waste pile after the first deal. This game is similar to St. Helena, but is easier because it has more columns and they are shorter.

House in the Woods
With Two Packs

This game is almost identical to *Clover Leaves* but a double pack is used, making a much bigger tableau consisting of thirty-two clusters of three cards each, with the eight Aces set up as foundations.

Cards are built upward on the foundations according to suit (Ace to King) and may be transferred from one auxiliary to another in descending sequence, exactly as in the *Clover Leaves* game. All rules of *Clover Leaves* apply.

Though this game takes longer, it is easier than *Clover Leaves* as the player often has choice of two identical cards (as 5S and 5S) while building on a foundation.

House on the Hill
Two Packs

This is like the game of *House in the Woods* but the foundations consist of four Aces, with one of each suit; and four Kings, also with one of each suit. The tableau has the usual thirty-two "leaves" of three cards each.

In building, cards from the tableau go in ascending order on the Aces (Ace up to King), but in descending order on the Kings (King down to Ace.) Also, in shifting cards from one auxiliary cluster to another, they can be placed in ascending order as well as descending, according to suit. Cards can also be moved from one foundation to another, which often aids to winning the game.

Sixes and Sevens

Two Packs

All Sixes and Sevens are removed from the double pack and formed into a 4 by 4 square. To the right, nine cards are dealt from the shuffled pack into a 3 by 3 square, like this:

6D	6D	6H	6H		KH	3S	9D
6C	6C	6S	6S		5H	JC	8C
7D	7D	7H	7H		9C	AD	JC
7C	7C	7S	7S				

The purpose is simple. The Sixes are foundations, on which cards are built in descending order, 6-5-4-3-2-A, according to each suit. The Sevens are foundations, for building in ascending order, 7-8-9-10-J-Q-K, by suit. Cards are taken from the tableau (on the right) and built on the foundations as stated.

With the tableau shown, the 5H would be built on a 6H; the 8C would be built on a 7C; and the 9C would be built on the 8C. Spaces in the tableau are then filled by dealing from the face-down stock. More builds are then made, if possible, and this goes on until play is blocked. Then, cards are dealt one by one from the stock into a face-up waste pile.

Any card from the stock can be built upon a proper foundation, and so can the top card of the waste pile. When more cards are built from the tableau, spaces can be filled by working back through the waste pile. This helps the player get at cards which would otherwise be lost.

The object is to build all foundations completely, winding up with eight Aces and eight Kings. It is difficult to do this in one try. Most players turn down the waste pile at the end of the deal and treat it as a new stock, going through a second time.

Egyptian Pyramids

Two Packs

Though similar to *Sixes and Sevens,* this is an interesting game in its own right. The Aces and Twos are removed from the pack, to form a hollow pyramid of sixteen cards. as:

		8H	JD			
	9S	4C	8H			
AH	7D	8H	QC	3D		2H

The Aces are foundations which are built upward in odd numbers, A-3-5-7-9-J-K, according to their suits. The Twos are foundations which are built up in even numbers, 2-4-6-8-10-Q. The smaller pyramid is the tableau and its cards are used for such building. The 3D would go on the AD; the 4C would go on the 2C.

Spaces are filled by dealing from the face-down stock, and cards can be built directly from the stock as well. When play is blocked, the stock is dealt into a face-up waste pile. The top card of that pile is always available for building or filling.

The stock can be dealt through twice if necessary.

Aztec Pyramids

Two Packs

players prefer it because the foundations come out equal. That is because the Kings are first removed from the double pack, reducing it from 104 to 96. The outer pyramid is dealt with Aces and Twos as foundations, and there are nine cards in the inner pyramid, so the tableau is the same as shown under *Egyptian Pyramids*.

Foundations, however, are built A-3-5-7-9-J and 2-4-6-8-10-Q. The absence of the Kings makes the game a little easier and many players limit the game to a single deal through the stock.

All Four Suits

One of the simplest of Solitaires, this seems easy at the start but can rapidly build to some exciting moments. The pack is shuffled and four cards are dealt in a square, as:

6H   KS

3C   JH

Any pair of the same suit is immediately eliminated and two cards dealt to replace them. In this case, the 6H and JH would be removed. Assume that the deal of the next two shows:

9S   KS

3C   5S

Here there is a choice of removing 9S and KS, or KS and 5S. Assume that 9S and KS are removed and two more cards are dealt:

AS   QC

3C   5S

In this case, both Spades and both Clubs could be removed, clearing the board, which means four cards must be dealt, as:

3D   8C

8H   2S

Since all the suits are different, none can be paired. However, when a player is blocked on suits, he is allowed to pair and remove cards of the same value, in this case, the 8C and 8H.

There are still times when the game can reach an absolute impasse, as with the following:

3D   QH

AC   2S

No paired suit there, and no paired value to the rescue, so the game is lost. To win, the entire pack of fifty-two cards must be dealt and paired away.

Marriages

This is a simple "pairing game" where only values count, and to be paired, cards must be side by side, one above the other, or corner to corner. This is easy to note in the following tableau, dealt with sixteen cards:

KC   2D   9S   5C

10H   3D   9C   AH

3C   QD   QS   JH

2S   JD   6S   QC

The 9S and 9C can be paired and removed; so can the 3D and 3C. The player has his choice of pairing and removing the QD and QS or the QS and QC.

Spaces are filled by moving cards up from the lower rows in order. The 5C would be moved in to replace the 9S, the 10H would go in the space left by the 5C, the AH would come over to the left of the second row, and so on. Any remaining vacancies (six in this case) are filled by dealing from the stock. Further pairing is made, cards are moved up.

Bingo

This Solitaire gets its name from its similarity to the popular *Bingo* game. It begins with a tableau of twenty-five cards in five rows of five cards each:

3H	9S	10C	KD	6D
AD	5D	QS	JC	10H
4C	4S	AC	2H	3D
KC	QS	JH	2D	8C
7C	10S	8D	5S	JS

The stock, containing twenty-seven cards, is held face down. Cards are then dealt one by one on to the tableau in an effort to make its cards show alternate colors; as Top Row, red, black, red, black, red; Second Row, black, red, black, red, black, and so on.

Only one card can be dealt on a card already showing, so the whole tableau is changed at the finish. Usually a player deals on opposite colors at the start, to get his rows established; for instance, he might deal the AH on the 10C and the 5C on the KD, to make the Top Row run red, black, red, black, red. But later, he can deal on red (as KH on 3H) or a black on black, (as 6C on 9S). Thus the final tableau may appear:

KH	6C	AH	5C	8H
2S	4D	KS	9D	6S
10D	7S	6H	3C	9H
AS	JD	9C	4H	2C
QH	3S	7H	8S	5H

There are two cards left over, the QD and the 7D. These are simply discarded during the course of the deal, if the player sees he can not place them without disturbing the alternating colors in the rows. These left-over cards are the crux of the game. A player may find himself down to three reds toward the finish, with no place to put one he loses.

The tableau should be studied at the outset, to see whether it is better to start the Top Row as red, black, red, black, red, or as black, red, black, red, black. This has a bearing on the rows that follow and therefore may make or break the game.

Bongo

This game is the same as *Bingo* but more difficult, as only fifty cards are used. First, discard a red and a black (as the AS and AH) and then proceed by dealing a tableau of twenty-five cards, as in *Bingo*. From then on, deal cards to make the rows show alternating colors.

In both *Bingo* and *Bongo* it is allowable to reshuffle the original tableau and deal again, if it looks too difficult. A second reshuffle is also allowed, but the third deal must stand.

Four-Leaf Clovers

Four-leaf clovers bring good luck and Number 13 stands for bad luck, so this game is really a combination of both. Your job is to keep one from neutralizing the other and eliminating you as well. Outside of that, it's very simple.

Shuffle the pack and deal out thirteen groups of four cards each, all face up and overlapping, so that you can see the cards beneath, but only the front card of each group can be played. If an Ace is available, it can be built as a foundation; a Two can go on that; then a Three and so on up.

This build does not have to follow suit, but there is just that one foundation. When it reaches a King, another Ace if built on top, and the whole pile begins to grow until the entire pack reads from foundation card up: A, 2, 3, 4, 5, 6, 7, 8, 9, 10, J, Q, K, A, 2, 3, 4, 5, 6, 7, 8, 9, 10, J, Q, K, A, 2, 3, 4, 5, 6, 7, 8, 9, 10, J, Q, K, A, 2, 3, 4, 5, 6, 7, 8, 9, 10, J, Q, K, A, 2, 3, 4, 5, 6, 7, 8, 9, 10, J, Q, K.

At least that's how it should be, but the problem is to get that far. Somehow, you must manage to release the lower petals of the four-leaf clovers, so as to have proper values ready when needed. Often, you may have to extricate an Ace just to get the big build under way.

This is done by transferring the front cards from one clover to another, releasing those below. You can place a card on another in ascending or descending value, as 6 on 7, 5 on 6, or 7 on 6, 8 on 7, whichever is most convenient. When you get up to a King, you can put an Ace on it; or you can put a King on an Ace in descending value. Thus you add petals or subtract them at will, but when a clover is fully plucked, it is gone to stay. So don't get rid of them too soon or you may shorten your game and lose out.

As the game proceeds, groups should be gradually fixed so that they ascend in value from the front petal down; then, it is easy to run out the last portion of the build, the final sequence from Ace up to King. Otherwise, play may be blocked.

Squared Away

This game is similar to *Four Leaf Clovers* but more difficult. Thirteen groups of four cards each are dealt face down, then squared into packets. The top card of each packet is turned up and play proceeds exactly as in *Four Leaf Clover*. A single foundation is built from Ace upward and cards are transferred from group to group in ascending or descending order.

But here the player does not know what lies beneath the top card of a group until he has transferred it. He then turns up the next card, possibly to his regret when he sees what it is. But he must stand by the transfer, whether good or bad. Wrong guesses may result in blocks.

Count Down

Remove the face cards (Kings, Queens, Jacks) from a pack and shuffle the rest. You then start playing Solitaire as if you were taking off on a space flight from Cape Kennedy. You count down, using "Ten, Nine, Eight, Seven, Six, Five, Four, Three, Two, One," dealing a card face up on each count, and then repeat the count down, using the whole 40-card pack.

Whenever you hit, as dealing an Eight on the count of "Eight", lay that card aside. You must make at least one hit during the deal, or the game is lost. If you hit, and you may score several, shuffle the rest of the pack and count down through it again. If you hit, you shuffle and deal again.

When you have less than ten cards, count down as far as you can, then turn the packet over and continue through. With seven cards, you would count "10, 9, 8, 7, 6, 5, 4" — turn over — "3-2-1-10-9-8-7." With four cards, you would count "10-9-8-7" — turn over — "6-5-4-3" — turn over — "2-1-10-9."

Hodge-Podge

A pack is shuffled and spread face down all over

the table so the cards are in hodge-podge fashion. A space is left in the center, however, large enough to receive four cards. The player takes a card from the hodge-podge and turns it face up, to represent one of four foundations, like this:

5C   *
*   *

The 5C becomes the foundation on which Clubs are to be built in ascending sequence, 5-6-7-8-9-10-J-Q-K-A-2-3-4. Another card is turned up, if it is the 6C it goes on the 5C; if it is another Five, it starts a foundation for its suit, which is built up in the same way.

Other cards are placed in four face-up piles as they are turned up. These are waste piles and their top cards are always available for building. So during the course of the game, it may appear as follows:

8C   5H
7D   10S
(Foundations)
3H   9D   9H   QS
(Waste Piles)

If the player should luckily draw the 8D from the hodge-podge, he could build it on the 7D, then move the 9D from its waste pile on to the 8D. Or, if he should draw the JS, he could build it on the 10S, and move the QS from its waste pile on to the JS. Either play would reveal a new card on a waste pile, or would clear the waste pile so other cards could go there.

After all cards have been drawn from the hodge-podge, a player can turn a waste pile face down and then turn up its cards one by one, building them if possible. Otherwise, he deals them into a fresh waste pile. He does this with each waste pile in turn. One deal through the waste piles is customary, but some players allow two. The object, of course, is to build all the foundations to their limit.

Jack Straws

This is a variant of *Hodge-Podge* in which the Jacks are the foundations, their piles running J-Q-K-A-2-3-4-5-6-7-8-9-10. The player can not start building until a Jack is drawn from the outspread cards, hence the game is often more difficult. Because of that, the player is always allowed to go through each waste pile twice. Otherwise, the game is identical with *Hodge-Podge*.

Double or Nothing
Two Packs

Here, two complete packs are used in a game of *Hodge-Podge* and space is made for eight center cards instead of only four. There are still four waste piles, however, so the tableau, during the course of the game, would take on an appearance like this:

8C	JH	10C	2H	5D	9S	QS
3S	(Tableau)	KH	5H	AC	2S	

(Waste Piles)

The rules are the same as *Hodge-Podge* with two deals allowed through each waste pile.

Aces and Kings

This game seems so simple that most people think they can succeed in a few tries. Instead, they are apt to go on and on, until they decide it can't be worked at all. Yet it can be, as will be explained.

Only eight cards are used, four Aces and four Kings. These are turned down and thoroughly mixed. Then they are dealt as follows: First card, from top of pack, face up on the table. Next card is moved face down from top of card to bottom. Next card, face up on table; next card, from top to bottom; and so on. The final card is simply turned face up on those already dealt.

The game is to make the cards fall in the order: Ace, King, Ace, King, Ace, King, Ace, King. But there is only one combination out of hundreds that will do it. So somewhere along the line it almost always goes astray, making this is one of the most difficult of Solitaires.

It's easy, of course, if you know the combination and set up the cards beforehand. Arrange the cards Ace, Ace, King, King, Ace, Ace, King, King, from top to bottom of the packet.

Order of Suits

This is similar to *Aces and Kings* but far more difficult. The Aces and Kings are shuffled face down, then dealt in the usual fashion: One up, one under, and so on. The purpose in this case is ti turn up Ace, King of one suit; then another; then a third; and finally a fourth, without a miss.

Obviously, you can be doing nicely with Ace, King, Ace, King, only to have one wrong suit spoil the whole thing. So the best way is to arrange the cards beforehand and prove to people that it really can be done. A good arrangement is AS, AC, KS, AD, AH, KC, KH, KD.

This comes out Ace-King of Spades, Ace-King of Hearts, Ace-King of Coubs, Ace-King of Diamonds. There are also other arrangements that will bring the suits out in different order.

Ace up to King

An even more difficult Solitaire involving the "one up, one under" deal is worked with thirteen cards, each of a different value, from Ace up to King. These are shuffled face down, then dealt as already described, the first up, the next under, and so on.

The purpose in this case is to bring up the cards in perfect rotation, Ace, Two, Three, Four, Five, Six, Seven, Eight, Nine, Ten, Jack, Queen, King. This may work out after a few thousand tries, but perhaps not even then!

So the best plan is to set it up, show it can be done, and let other people find out how impossible it can be. The correct set-up, form top to bottom of the packet, runs: A, Q, 2, 8, 3, J, 4, 9, 5, K, 6, 10, 7.

Even Steven

From a shuffled pack, deal two cards face up side by side, and if their total is an even number, discard them. In this game, Ace = 1 and other cards run according to value, up to Jack = 11, Queen = 12, King = 13. So the 6H and QD would be an even pair (6 + 12) as would the K H and 5H (13 + 5 = 18).

If a pair proves odd, like 4S and 9C (4 + 9 = 13) or JC and 2H (11 + 2 = 13) they must stay on the table. In that case, a third card is dealt beside the second, and if their total is even, they are removed:

but if odd, they stay. As the game progresses, the board may be frequently cleared as more cards are dealt, or the line may increase, like this:

5C   4D   AH   3C   QC   7C

Here, the pairs add, $5 + 4 = 9$; $4 + 1 = 5$; $1 + 3 = 4$; $3 + 12 = 15$; $12 + 7 = 19$. All totals being odd, they must stay. However, should the 7C be followed by a single odd card, as the 5D, their total would be even ($7 + 5 = 12$) and that pair would be eliminated. Another card would then be dealt alongside the QC, to see if it would add up to "odd" or "even."

The purpose of the game is eliminate all the cards by means of even totals, making it exciting down to the last card.

Criss-Cross

A very simple tableau is used in this easy but exciting Solitaire. From a shuffled pack, five cards are dealt in crosswise fashion, face up. Here is an example:

6H

4S   KD   9H

10D

The next card of the pack is turned up and if it matches a card in the tableau in value, the two are removed and laid aside, face down. In this case, if the 9C should be turned up, it would take the 9H and both would be discarded. Another card is then dealt in hope of a match (such as KC with KD) but if an odd card turns up (such as the 2C) it is used to fill the space and keep the cross intact.

When no spaces remain, an odd card goes on the center of the tableau, as JS on KD, which becomes a waste pile, though it is still part of the tableau. Any time a space occurs because of a new match, a card is moved from the center pile to fill the gap.

This frequently results in another match in the tableau itself. If not, the player keeps on dealing as before. If he eventually matches up all cards and clears the board, he wins the game.

Note: All matches must be pairs only, never three of a kind, as that will leave an odd unmatchable card at the finish.

Mix them and Match Them

An entire pack of 52 cards is dealt in pairs, one card above the other.

Any pairs that match in suit or value are removed from the tableau. The rest are gathered and reshuffled, then dealt again.

Again, pairs matching in suit or value are eliminated, and the remaining cards are gathered and dealt, possibly coming out as:

2D 7D 8S KD 9H KC
5D 9S 7H 4D 9C QC

Here, pairs 2D-5D, KD-4D, 9H-9C, KC-QC would be eliminated, leaving only four cards to be dealt again. If the player should match those, 7D-7H in value, and 8S-9S in suit, he would win. If he should fail to pair them properly, he would lose.

Ten — Twenty — Thirty

A fast, exciting Solitaire in which only values count, with suits playing no part. Beginning with Ace as 1, cards run in value 2, 3, 4, 5, 6, 7, 8, 9, 10 with Jacks, Queens and Kings as 10 each.

Start dealing cards in a row from left to right, adding their values as you do. But this is really done by counting backward, as each new card appears. Thus a Five followed by a Nine would be 14; an Eight next would be 17 (9 + 8) or 22 (5 + 9 + 8)

The purpose is to eliminate groups of two or more cards which add exactly to 10, 20 or 30.

Five, Nine, Eight, King, Seven, Jack, Two, Queen, Eight, Nine, You could eliminate the Jack, Queen, Eight, because they total 30. (10 + 2 + 10 +8).

Add Up Tens

Eliminate Kings, Queens and Jacks from the pack leaving a total of thirty-six cards, which are rated according to value, Ace for one, up to Nine for nine. Deal nine of these cards into a 3 by 3 square, as:

8   6   7

8   9   A

4   7   5

If any of these cards pair up to total 10, they are taken from the tableau. In this case, the Six and Four would be eliminated, as they total 10. So would the Nine and Ace, which total 10. To win, the 36-card pack must be paired off completely.

Totals of Fifteen

Only nine cards are used in this Solitaire, one of

each value from Ace up to Nine. The object is to deal them in a 3 by 3 square, with every row totaling 15, across, down or diagonally. This is more of a puzzle than a game, as only a few of thousands of combinations will bring the required result, as shown here:

2	7	6
9	5	1
4	3	8

Pick Out Pictures

A good Solitaire for children. The pack is shuffled and cards are dealt in four heaps of four each, sixteen cards in all. If any picture cards (Kings, Queens Jacks) appear, they are laid aside and other cards are dealt to replace them.

The tableau of sixteen cards is gathered and added to the pack, which is given another shuffle. Again, four rows of four cards are dealt, eliminating picture cards. This is done a third time and finally a fourth. To win, all twelve picture cards must be eliminated by the end of the fourth deal.

Digging for Diamonds

Another simple game of elimination. Shuffle the pack and deal three rows of five cards each, all face up. From these, remove any Diamonds that appear in the tableau and deal other cards to fill the spaces, still removing any Diamonds until no more appear.

Gather the final fifteen cards, shuffle them in the pack and deal fifteen cards again, in the same way. After digging out all Diamonds that you can, gather up the cards and deal a third tableau and last.

Four Square

The four Aces are removed from the pack, which is then dealt to form a tableau of sixteen cards, all face up, the aces being placed outside the corners:

AD   AH

JC	3H	5C	5C	5S
	9S	KC	10D	2H
	4S	QC	JD	7H
	2S	8C	8S	JH
	7D	6C	QH	3C

AS   AC

The Aces serve as foundations, and cards are taken from the tableau and built upward on the Aces according to suit. In this illustration, the 2H would go on the AH and the 3H on the 2H. The 2S would then be built on the AS. That would make three spaces in the tableau; those are filled by new cards dealt from the stock.

When play is blocked, cards are dealt from the stock into a face up waste pile. A card can be built directly from the stock onto a foundation, and the uppermost card of the waste pile may be built or used to fill a gap in the tableau, this being the most important part of the game.

Five by Five

Similar to *Four Square* but much easier. A tableau is formed by dealing five rows of five cards each, or twenty-five in all. If any Aces appear, they are taken from the tableau and placed in a row above to form foundations.

More cards are dealt from the stock for building or to fill the tableau. The rest go into the waste pile which can be played back to tableau or foundations. This game is very easy, but if the Aces are slow in coming up, it may seem a sure loss until the end.

Tricky Thirteen

Simple but tantalizing, this game begins with dealing a tableau of 13 cards, preferably in rows of 4-5-4, though any convenient arrangement is allowable. All cards are dealt face up and any Aces are removed and set as foundations in a special row above. If any cards can be built on the Aces in ascending sequence according to suit, that is done.

From the face-down pack or stock, new cards are dealt to fill spaces as they occur in the tableau; these, too, are built on foundations whenever possible. Then, when the tableau is filled, the player must start weeding out any duplicate values that appear there, putting them in a single face-up waste pile below the tableau.

As example, with the 6H and 6C in the tableau, the Heart can be put in the waste pile and the Club left in the tableau or vice versa. With the JC, JS, JD in the tableau, first one and later another must be transferred to the waste pile. From the start, choice is important, for it is wise to discard duplicates that are less likely to be needed in earlier builds.

In the example, one Jack could be discarded, then another, rather than a Six. By keeping the Six in the tableau, it may be possible to retain it until it can be built on a foundation. But when a card goes into the waste pile, it is not lost. The top card of the waste pile can always be built directly on a foundation; and it can also be brought back to a space in the tableau, once its duplicate is gone from there, due to a build.

Suppose the 6H and 6C are in the tableau and that one must be discarded, so the 6H is put in the waste pile. The gap in the tableau is filled with the 5C from the stock and it happens that the Club foundation is already up to the 4C. So the 5C is built on the foundation; then the 6C. There is no longer a

Six in the tableau, so the 6H can be returned there.

In this way, it is possible to work back through the waste pile, regaining cards that have been buried there. But high values block low values that are beneath them in the waste pile, especially when both are of the same suit. This is something to guard against when possible.

With a single deal through the pack, this game can prove very difficult and is sometimes lost in the early stages. So once it becomes hopeless, due to blockage of low values in the waste pile, it is best to start over, unless a player decides to include a second deal.

In that case, he completes the first deal and turns the waste pile face down, intact, to form a new stock from which the deal is continued with play as given.

Down the Line

The aces are discarded from the pack in this game, reducing the required cards from 52 to 48. The Kings, Queens and Jacks are set in three rows of four each, as foundations, while a square of nine (3 by 3) is dealt as a face-up tableau.

Cards are taken from the tableau and built on the foundations in the order King, Ten, Nine, Eight; Queen, Seven, Six, Five; Jack, Four, Three, Two. These sequences must be in suit, as in the following illustration:

KH	KD	KS	KC
QH	QD	QS	QC
JH	JD	JS	JC

6H	10C	3D
9D	7C	2S
9S	4C	6C

The 10C would go on the KC; the 7C on the QC; the 6C on the 7C; the 4C on the JC. That would leave four spaces in the tableau, which are filled by dealing cards from the face-down stock, hoping to continue play. When play is blocked, cards are dealt from the stock into a face-up waste pile, with the top card of that pile always available for play.

Only one deal is allowable, as the game may prove fairly easy, ending with foundations showing Eights, Fives and Twos.

Marguerite

This is the original form of *Down The Line* and is virtually the same game, except that the foundations are set in the form of a letter "M" and the tableau as a letter "A", representing the beginning of the name "Marguerite" This makes a nice arrangement for players who are artistically inclined.

Five and Ten

Eighty Cards

Two full packs are required for this Solitaire, but all face cards are discarded, so that suits run only from Ace to Ten, making 80 cards in all. The Fives and Sixes are dealt face up as foundations and below those a row of four "auxiliary cards," as shown here:

5C	5C	6C	6C
5D	5D	6D	6D
5S	5S	6S	6S
5H	5H	6H	6H
8D	2D	4S	9C

From the auxiliaries, the player builds down on the Fives to the Aces (5-4-3-2-A) according to suits. He also builds up on the Sixes to the Tens (6-7-8-9-10) according to suits. In the illustration, the only possible build would be to put the 4S on a 5S. A gap thus formed in the auxiliary row is immediately fill-ed by dealing a card from the face-down stock.

A card from the stock can also be built directly on a foundation (as 7D on a 6D) but when no play is possible, it must be dealt into a face-up waste pile.

The Serpent
Two Packs

An early form of *Five and Ten*, this starts with Fives and Sixes as face-up foundations, but they are dealt end to end, forming a long spiral that resem-bles a coiled serpent, hence the name of this Solitaire. Four auxiliary cards are dealt below the serpent.

The play is the same as *Five and Ten*, the Fives be-ing built down by the suits (5-4-3-2-A) and the Sixes up by suits (6-7-8-9-10-Q-K.) Note that the Jacks are absent from the upward progression, as they are simply eliminated during course of play, being add-ed to the end of the serpent to continue its long coil. Odd cards go in the face up waste pile.

Descending from Fives to Aces is easier than as-cending from Sixes to Kings, because of the two ex-tra cards in the upward arrangement. If blocked at the end of the first deal, the player may turn the waste pile face down and deal through it again.

Garden of Eden
Two Packs

A cross between *Five and Ten* and the Serpent, rep-resenting a transition from one to the other. The same foundations (Fives and Sixes) are used, building down by suits on Fives to Aces (5-4-3-2-A) and up on Sixes to Tens (6-7-8-9-10).

As Jacks appear, they are added as new foundations, each representing a serpent. Each Jack (serpent) the player builds a Queen (Eve) and a King (Adam) of the same suit as the Jack.

The Letter "T"

Two Packs

Four Aces, of different suits, are taken from the pack and arranged in a column. Four Kings, also of different suits, are set on each side of the top Ace, forming a Letter "T". These serve as foundations, Aces to be built up to Kings according to suit, and Kings down to Aces, by suits. Below, twelve cards are dealt face up as a tableau. Here is the result:

KH	KD	AS	KS	KC
		AD		
		AC		
		AH		

9D	7H	QS	8C	
	4D	9D	5C	JS
	2C	QD	7H	10S

Immediate builds would be 2C on AC; QD on KD; QS on KS; JS on QS; 10S on JS.

Twelve more cards are then dealt, one on each card or space in the tableau, covering any that are already there. So the tableau becomes auxiliary piles. Any cards on top of the piles are available for play, and afterward twelve more are dealt on the piles. This continues for eight deals or 96 cards in all.

The piles may then be gathered, shuffled and redealt; and this can be done for a third deal, if necessary. During the building, cards can be moved from one foundation to another. That is, if the AD has been built up to the 5D and KD has been built down to the 6D, the 5D can be moved from the Ace foundation on to the 6D belonging to the KD foundation.

Rotation

A pack is shuffled and the player begins to deal cards in a face-up heap, continuing until an Ace appears, it is used for a foundation as well; and any Two goes on an Ace, regardless of suit.

Similarly, a Three is built on a Two, a Four on a Three, and so on upward, the purpose being simply to form four piles running up from Ace to King, suits making no difference. At the finish of the deal, the waste pile may be turned over and dealt through as a new stock. A third such deal is also allowable, but that is all.

Doubled Rotation

Also played with a single pack, this is regular *Rotation* but with Kings also used as foundations, when they come along. Aces are built upward and Kings downward, until they meet. There are eight foundations in all, which makes the doubled game easier, but because of that, it must be done in a single deal through the pack.

Follow the Leader

An unusual Solitaire utilizing only half a pack. To start, a red King and a black King are removed and laid face up on the table. These are the "leaders." The pack is shuffled and twenty-four cards are dealt in a face-down packet.

The player now deals followers face-down on the face-up leaders, trying to guess whether the followers are red or black as he deals them.

At the end of the deal, he turns the heaps face up and discards all reds from the black group and all blacks from the red group. This might leave him six blacks and seven reds. He shuffles these together and deals them on the leaders, but now he knows how many are blacks and how many are reds, so he can gauge his deal accordingly.

Again, he turns up the cards and weeds and shuffles and deals for the third time. They are then turned up and if only black cards are with the black King and only reds with the red King, the game is won. In this instance, two cards would finally be dealt on the black King, four on the red King.

First: KC 9H 5D 3C JC 9S QC 3H 8S 10S QD
       KH AD 4C 8C 2D 7H 7C 9D AH 8H JS
                                  AC 4S JH
Second: KC 2D AC. 3H 10S 10S AD JH
        KH QD 8H 9S 4S 7H 5D 7C
Third: KC 10S AC·
        KH 8H 5D QD 7H

Out of This World

This is played like *Follow the Leader* but with a full pack. All four Kings are removed and twenty-four followers are dealt on the KC, representing Red, and the KH, representing Black, with the player guessing at the color or each face-down card.

But instead of stopping there, the player continues to deal, using tthe KD (Red) and KS (Black) as new leaders, so twenty-four followers also go on those. He turns up the cards in the first set, weeds reds and blacks, shuffles, and deals again in the usual fashion. Then he does the same with the cards in the second.

A third weed and deal follows, with the result be-

ing that the player may win with one set, even if he
loses with the other, though he tries to win both.

Ups and Downs

Two Packs

The Aces are taken from a double pack and form-
into a set of eight cards to serve as foundations.
Eight other cards are dealt face up to form a similar
set at the right, this being the tableau, as illustrated:

AD	AD	JD	2H
AC	AC	4C	8C
AH	AH	9H	6C
AS	AS	7C	3D

Cards can be built upward on the foundations according to suits, so in this case, the 2H could be
built on one AH, leaving a space. Also, cards may
be arranged in downward sequence, by suits, on the
auxiliary piles composing the tableau. So the 7C
could be put on the 8C and 6C on the 7C, leaving
two more spaces.

Such spaces are promptly filled by dealing from
the stock, so that more builds and moves can be
made. When such play is blocked, cards are dealt
from the face down stock to form a face-up waste
pile, with its top card always available. Builds can
be made directly from stock or waste pile to foundations and it is better to fill spaces in the tableau
from the waste pile, rather than from the stock.

Quick Turnover

A novel and intriguing Solitaire, in which sixteen
cards are dealt face down to from a 4 by 4 square:

.   .   .   .

.   .   .   .

.   .   .   .

.   .   .   .

On these, sixteen more cards are dealt face up, no

attention being paid to value or suit, but only to colors. The result may look like this:

R R B R
B R R R
B R B R
R R B B

The purpose is to show sixteen cards of the same color, making the tableau all red or all black. So the player turns over two cards as one, wherever it might help that purpose. If he doesn't like what turns up, he may turn the same pair over, reversing them to their original status.

Sometimes the game is won on the first deal, but if not, the player must deal sixteen cards face up on the tableau as it stands, forming a new set of colors. Again, each pile may be turned over as required in an effort to bring up sixteen all alike in color.

Even is the player fails the, he still may win. He has four cards left in the stock, and these may be placed face up on different piles.

Push Pin

This is a rapid and exciting Solitaire involving a continuous deal through the pack. The player starts a face-up row and whenever a single card or two cards come between a pair of the same suit or value, the intervening card or cards are pushed away an the row is closed. Here is an illustration:

6D   8C   9C   3H   JS   9D

Since the 9C and 9D are the same in value, the 3H and JS are pushed away. The row is closed to from:

6D   8C   9C   9D

The 6D and 9D are the same in suit, so the 8C and 9C are pushed away, leaving only two cards, the 6D and 9D.

If more than two cards lie between a matching pair, they cannot be removed, unless all the intervening cards are of one suit; then they can be pushed away all at once. Here is a case:

6D   9D   8S   JC   2C   5C   6C   KC   9S

All the Clubs can be pushed away from between the 8S and 9S, which match in suit. The 8S would then be alone between the 9D and 9S, which match in value, so the 8S could be pushed out. The line would then run: 6D 9D 9S.

Push and Pull

Two Packs

This Solitaire is about the same as *Push Pin*, but two packs are used, making it a longer game and sometimes stretching out the line of cards until it is very long. The rules of *Push Pin* apply as given, but with one addition, as follows:

With the double pack, every card has a duplicate. Whenever such a pair happens to come side by side, as the JD next to the JD, or the 5S next to the 5S, both cards can be pulled from the line. Hence the difference between "push" and "pull", although in each case, it is simply an elimination of cards.

Anna

Two Packs

This early form of *Ups and Downs* has interesting points and gains its name from the peculiar form of the tableau, which consists of eight face up cards dealt in the form of a letter A, for "Anna". The foundations are eight Jacks, which are dealt at the right during the course of play. They form a letter N, the second letter in "Anna."

Cards are taken from the tableau and built on

foundations in descending sequence, according to suit, so each foundation eventually runs J-10-9-8-7-6-5-4-3-2-A-K. Note that the Queen is not included, which is the oddity of this game. The tableau cards are moved from one pile to another, but in ascending sequence, according to suits; spaces being filled from the stock or waste pile as in *Ups and Downs*.

This ascending sequence can start from a King, running K-A-2-3 and so on, up to Jack. But again, Queens are not included in the sequence. They figure in the game, however, for when a Queen appears in the original tableau, it kills that pile entirely. Similarly, when a Queen is dealt into a space it also means a dead pile. Queens must be dealt as they come along, so play becomes more limited as the game proceeds.

Because of the "dead" Queens, three deals are allowed through the pack. If successful, the original tableau will consist of eight lone Queens, while the foundations will be topped by eight Jacks.

Elimination

Four cards are taken from the pack, each representing a suit, and they are set in a face-up row:

D   C   H   S

The pack is then shuffled and the player deals four heaps, one for each indicator, the deal being made card by card, heap by heap. These cards are dealt face down; then each is turned up and all cards of its suit are eliminated.

Thus, from the heap under "D" (a Diamond) all Diamonds would be removed; under "C", all Clubs; under "H" all Hearts; under "S" all Spades. Values have no significance.

The remainng cards are gathered and again dealt in rotation below the indicators. Another elimination follows. The same is done with a third deal, and a fourth, if necessary. To win, the player must eliminate all cards of one suit; which suit, does not matter. This must be done by the end of the fourth deal.

Daisy Petals

From a shuffled pack, eight cards are dealt in a face down circle to represent the petals of a daisy. These are turned up one by one, and are matched for color, a red with a red; a black with black, If all the petals can be paired in that fashion, the player wins. If the player is left with a red and a black, he loses.

To make the game more difficult, three "daisies" may be dealt, each with eight "petals". Each is "plucked" in turn, and to win, the player must successfully match the petals of each daisy in the chain.

Spell Them Through

More a puzzle tha a game, this consists of dealing three cards from a face-down pack, spelling "A-C-E" for Ace and turning up the third card. If it is an Ace, three more cards are dealt, spelling "T-W-O" and if aTwo turns up on the letter "O", the spelling is continued with "T-H-R-E-E" and on through the pack to "K-I-N-G'"

This result is almost impossible, so this is more fun to arrange the pack beforehand and work it as a demonstration, showing that it can be done. Simply put all the Aces together at the top of the pack; beneath those, the Twos; then the Threes; and so on.

Speller's Choice

This is an intriguing Solitaire, based on *Spell Them Through*. It allows for considerable foresight, as the player has a choice of "spells." The pack is shuffled and the first three cards dealt face up. If the third card is an Ace, the player can spell "A-C-E", he could spell it "T-W-O" laying the Two aside. He can do the same with S-I-X for Six, and T-E-N for Ten.

If none of those values should appear, a fourth card can be dealt face up. If a Four, the player can spell the cards as "F-O-U-R" and lay the Four aside. He can do the same with F-I-V-E for Five, N-I-N-E for Nine, J-A-C-K for Jack, or K-I-N-G for King.

Even if he misses one of those, the player can deal a fifth card and if it is a Three, he spells "T-H-R-E-E", laying the card aside. He can do the same with S-E-V-E-N for Seven, E-I-G-H-T for Eight, or Q-U-E-E-N for Queen. He then proceeds to deal three more face-up cards, endeavoring to hit another value in the same way, and so on through the pack, using each value only once.

This game seems easy but is quite difficult so after a "miss" it is best to gather the waste pile, shuffle and continue to deal a second and a third time. Even then, it is hard to win!

Color Sense

An easy but exciting game. A shuffled pack is dealt into two face-down piles. The top cards are turned up and if they match in color, as both red or both black, they are placed in a special pile. If they do not match, they are simply discarded.

After going through the pack in this fashion, the special pile of matched pairs is thoroughly shuffled and dealt into two piles, as before. Top cards are turned up and matched or rejected. The special pile is shuffled and the player goes through the process for the third time; then a fourth and a fifth.

Sixty-Fours

This is exactly the same as *Color Sense* but with a special pack of sixty-four cards as used in the game of Bezique and some forms of Pinochle. Such a pack has duplicates of all cards running from Ace down to Seven, and it can be made up by simply combining the necessary cards from two packs.

The player matches them for color, keeps the cards that match, and goes through the process five times. The advantage of this game is that dividing 64 by halves brings 32, 16, 8, 4.

Around the Circle

In this Solitaire, face cards are removed and the remainder of the pack is shuffled. Twelve cards are then dealt face up to form a circle like a clock dial.

The player turns down any card he wants, as the 8D, noting its value as he does. He counts that number around the circle, in either direction, until he reaches another card. In this, he might count clockwise, his total of eight ending on the 3S.

For convenience, the player turns each card face down before counting from it. His purpose is to turn down all the cards in the circle, by always ending his count on a face-up card.

Change About

In *Change About,* if the player fails, he can switch positions of different cards and start again. Here is an illustration:

```
        3D                          3D
   AD        6H              AD          6H
  4C           5D          4C               5D
5C    "X"    10C      5C      "Y"         4H
  8S         4H            8S          10C
    7D    9S                  6C      9S
      6C                          7D
```

Suppose the player turns down the 3D in Dial X and counts counterclockwise to 5C, 4H, 3D. He is back at the start, so play is blocked. So he transposes the 4H and 10C, also the 6C and 7D, as in Dial Y. His counterclockwise count would then run, 3D, 5C, 10C, 7D, AD, 4C. There, he can go clockwise to 5D, 6C, 6H. From there, play is blocked either way, so other changes will be needed.

Reverse the Colors

Similar to *Change About,* but more difficult, this game is played with the same dial, but with one specially added rule. When a red card appears in the circle, the move from that card must be clockwise; from a black card, the move is always counterclockwise.

This limits the player's choice in making transpo-
sitions, but he can come to decisions more quickly,
and may soon learn if the tableau is unplayable. On
that account, many players prefer *Reverse the Colors*
to other games of that particular type.

Suit Yourself

In this game, thirteen foundations are used, running from Ace up to King, all in the same suit. The
pack is shuffled, held face down and the top card is
turned up. It determines the suit, thus the 5C would
mean Club foundations throughout. So the first card
is set at its position in an imaginary line, in this case
fifth, and the deal continues.

Each Club that appears goes in its foundation
spot (in order, A-2-3-4-5-6-7-8-9-10-J-Q-K) and
once a foundation has been started, cards of that
same value are dealt upon it, but they must be of
the opposite color. Thus, the 5C would have to be
covered by the 5D or 5H.

Cards that cannot be built are dealt in a face-up
waste pile, which can be used for building, its top
card being available. This game is difficult to win in
one deal, so the player may turn over the waste pile
and deal through it again, as a new stock. The second try is often very easy.

Jacks in Array
Two Packs

This is *Suit Yourself* with a double pack, ending
up with piles of eight cards each, all in alternating
colors, but with only twelve such foundations. The

reason is, the Jacks are eliminated, so the foundations simply run A-2-3-4-5-6-7-8-9-10-Q-K. The
Jacks may be in the pack to start, but whenever one
appears, it is dealt in a line of its own, with no regard for basic suit or alternating colors. So the Jacks
simply form an array of onlookers. Regular piles all
start building from one suit, as in *Suit Yourself.*

Floradora

Two Packs

Similar to Lucas and St. Helena, this Solitaire
gains its name from the famous Floradora Sextette of
the early 1900's. In one way it is more difficult than
kindred Solitaires; in another way, easier. So it should
be considered as a game in its own right.

The player deals a tableau of six columns of six
cards each, representing the sextette, as illustrated:

8H	5D	10C	7D	2H
AC	QC	4D	JH	5C
5D	4S	JC	JS	6S
6S	7D	7H	10S	8H
AH	9C	9D	4H	8D
10D	2H	JD	QS	AS

Note that there are no Kings in the tableau. They
are discarded as they appear during the deal, so that
the Queens, representing the Floradora Girls, will be
the final cards built upon foundations which begin
with Aces and run upward according to suit (A-2-3-
4-5-6-7-8-9-10-J-Q).

To get at the Aces, the player can transfer cards
from the bottom row, packing them on others in descending sequence. Only those cards (which are usually overlapped) are available, but they do not have

to follow suit in this game, which is the great advantage. When a row is used up, any card can be moved into the space.

A few plays will make the precedure plain. The AS is placed as a foundation. The JD goes on the QS, the 10D on the JD. The AH is placed as a foundation; the 2H is built on the AH. The 9C is moved on the 10D; the 8D goes on the 9C; the 7D on the 8D; the 6S on the 7D; the 5D on the 6S. The AC is set as a foundation and the 8H can be put on the 9D later, to make a space.

When moves are blocked, or reserved for later, the player deals from the face-down stock into a face-up waste pile, using available cards for building or packing as they come along. Any Kings are dealt into their own special pile, so they can admire the Floradora Girls as the foundations build up to Queens. Only one deal through the pack.

Ten Little Indians

Two Packs

This is a cross between St. Helena and Canfield. A tableau of ten columns with four cards each is dealt as in St. Helena, but the first three cards of each column go gace down, only the final row being face up as illustrated here:

```
*    *    *    *    *    *    *    *    *    *

*    *    *    *    *    *    *    *    *    *

*    *    *    *    *    *    *    *    *    *
```

6H   4C   AS   KD   JC   4D 10H   QD   3S   8S

Any Aces are used to start foundations, building up to Kings of their suit. Cards may be shifted from column to column, singly and in descending sequence of alternating colors. In the illustration, the JC

would go on the QD, and the 10H on the JC. Also
the 3S on the 4D. Face down cards are then turned
up to replace those removed, becoming available for
play as in Canfield.

Groups of cards can be transferred, also as in
Canfield, and this applies to portions of groups.
Thus a sequence like 8D - 7C - 6D could be moved
on to the 9C or 9S; or the 7C - 6D could go on the
8H; or just the 6D could be shifted to the 7S. The
stock is dealt on to a waste pile as in St. Helena.

Forty and Eight
Two Packs

This Solitaire is named after the famous French
freight cars of World War I, that held forty men or
eight horses. Whether any soldiers played it while in
transit is a question.

All rules given under St. Helena should be followed, except for the dealing of the original tableau. Instead of dealing ten face up columns of four cards
each, the player deals eight face up columns of five
cards each. The columns (8) stand for the eight
horses; the total number of cards in the tableau (40)
for the forty men.

Famous Fifty
Two Packs

A fairly modern form of St. Helena, this Solitaire
follows the rules of that game exactly, even to the
dealing of ten columns in the tableau. The only difference is the number of cards in each column. In St.
Helena, there are four to a column, in Famous Fifty,

there are five to a column, making fifty in all. As
with St. Helena, all cards are dealt face up, in overlapping form.

This game was named in honor of the Famous
Fifty baseball fans, a group who annually travelled
by special Pullman cars to see the World Series games,
hence it is quite a contrast to the box-car version of
Forty and Eight.

Thermometer

Though simple, this is exciting, making it a good
juvenile game. Seven cards are dealt face down in a
column, to represent a thermometer. An extra card,
like the 5C, is dealt face up beside the central card,
to represent the temperature:

*

*

*

*   5C

*

*

*

The player turns up the card beside the 5C. If it
is a black, the temperature rises and the 5C is pushed up to the card above. If a red, the temperature
falls, and the 5C is brought down a peg, unless the
red happens to be a Five (like the 5H or 5D) in which
case, it counts as a rise.

As the temperature rises and falls, new cards are
dealt face up from the pack on the cards already
turned up, and these new cards denote further rise
and fall. The player wins if the temperature card
rises out the top, he loses if it drops out the bottom.

Freezing Point

This is exactly the same as Thermometer, except for the number of cards in the column. In this game, there are eleven, each representing teń degrees: 100, 90, 80, 70, 60, 50, 40, 30, 20, 10, 0. The player sets his temperature card at 30 (four cards, up from the bottom) as that is approximately the freezing point. Play proceeds as with Thermometer, with the player's purpose being to go above the 100° mark. If he falls below zero instead, he loses. In this game, the odds are against the player winning.

Canfield Junior

This game was designed for younger players who would like to win occasionally at standard Canfield. It is the regular game but with more liberal rules as to packing cards in downward sequence on auxiliary piles.

The player starts by dealing the usual tableau for Canfield, seven piles consisting of 1, 2, 3, 4, 5, 6, and 7 cards respectively, all face down except the top card of each pile:

```
2S      *     *     *     *     *     *
6D      *     *     *     *     *
              KH    *     *     *     *
                    7C    *     *     *
                          3C    *     *
                                QH    *
                                      8S
```

Cards are moved from one pile to another to form descending sequences, regardless of suit or color. Here, the 2C is packed on the 3C; the 6D on the 7C and both on the 8S; the QH goes on the KH and both can be moved to fill the gap left by the 2S. Cards are then turned up on the five vacated heaps, offering chances for new transfers.

In regular Canfield, only the 6D could have been put on the 7S because of the alternating color rule, so the liberality of the Junior game is very apparent.

Whenever Aces appear, they are used as foundations toward building up to Kings, but his must be according to suit as in standard Canfield. Single cards and portions of sequences can be moved from pile to pile, as well as entire sequences. Cards are dealt from the stock into a waste pile, and these can be built or packed whenever they appear. Only one such deal in allowable.

Rat Race

A red card and a black card are taken from a pack to represent two racers. The pack is shuffled and twelve cards are dealt in a face down row, to serve as posts along a race track. The racing "rats" are placed to the left, one above and one below, as illustrated:

5H

　　*　*　*　*　*　*　*　*　*　*　*　*

9S

A card is dealt face up from the pack. If a red card, the Red Rat (5H) is moved to the first post; if a black, the Black Rat (9S) is moved. More cards are turned up from the pack and moves are made accordingly, until one racer reaches the final post and its color is turned up, sending it across the line.

As a Solitaire, the player wins if the top racer goes out first; if the bottom racer goes out first, he loses. If he wants, he can choose his color beforehand and set it as the "top rat." With two players, Rat Race can be treated as a competitive game.

Double Rat Race
Two Packs

Also known as Rat Pack, this also has twelve face-down cards as posts along the track, but there are four racing rats, each a Jack of a different suit, two above and below. Instead of going by colors, each moves when its own suit is turned up. This game is slower, but what it lacks in excitment, it makes up for with suspense. It is also harder to win, as the top Jack — whatever its suit — must come in first. The illustration shows a race in progress with the "top rat" out ahead of the Pack.

                              JD

    JH

*   *   *   *   *   *   *   *   *   *   *   *

              JC

        JS

Some players continue on after a "win" in hopes of bringing the four rats across the finish line in order 1, 2, 3, 4 from the top. In the illustration this would mean JD, JH, JC, JS. Four persons can play Double Rat Race on a competitive basis.

Three Card Monte

Four packets are made up containing nine cards each, six Blacks and three Reds. Each packet is shuffled separately, then its cards are dealt face up in three rows. The object is to have the three Red cards show up in a single row, horizontal, vertical or diagonal. These types are illustrated below:

JC 7H 4C	10S KS 3C	JS AS AD
2C 5D QS	9D JD 8H	7C QD 5C
6S 3H 9C	AC 5S 10C	KH KC 3S

These look easy, but they are really difficult, as in many other combinations, Reds fail to line up. Any packet that shows a row of three Reds is laid aside, and the remaining packets are shuffled separately and dealt again. The player has three such deals in which to line up the Reds in every packet.

Remember, *four* packets are used, with 36 cards in all, but the player is only allowed *three* deals in which to win.

Extrasensory Perception

Solitaire goes scientific in this game, which is based on tests made at Duke University. There, they use cards with five different symbols in a 25-card pack containing five of each type. But a similar result can be had with a packet of 16 playing cards, four of each suit.

The player shuffles the packet face down, then draws off the top card and tries to visualize its suit, as Diamonds. He lays that card face down to start a Diamond pile and tries to name the next card the same way. Continuing through the packet, he winds up with four heaps of four cards for each suit, Diamonds, Hearts, Clubs, Spades.

He then turns up the heaps to see how right he was. By the law of averages, he should hit one in each heap, or 4 out of 16. Anything consistently better than that is "evidential" as the ESP experts say. As a Solitaire, a player can go through the packet twenty-five times, anything over 100 hits as a win.

Two or more players can work with separate packets in competition, the highest at the end of twenty-five times being the winner of the contest. Some players like to use "target cards", one of each suit, face up, on which they deal the cards.

Four of a Kind

This is a form of the standard ESP game, using four cards of four different values, as the Aces, Fives, Tens and Kings. Some players like this better, as they can visualize the spots or face cards more clearly than the suits. The game is played and scored exactly as with Extrasensory Perception. The only difference is that the player counts one for every Ace he calls correctly; and the same for every Five, Ten, or King, suits being disregarded. No target cards are used in this form of the game.

Crossed Thoughts

By combining both forms of ESP, a player can really tax his wits. In this Solitaire, he used four Aces, Fives, Tens and Kings, but as he mentally weighs each card; he tries to visualize it completely, as the Ace of Hearts, Ten of Diamonds.

On the table, he pictures four columns, one for each suit, and four rows, one for each value. He then places each card at the junction where he thinks it belongs. Here is an illustration:

	Clubs	Diamonds	Hearts	Spades
Ace				(AS)
Five		(5D)		
Ten	(10C)		(10H)	
King				

The player has so far visualized four cards, as indicated in the brackets. After he has placed all sixteen, he will turn them up and tally the columns for suits, the cross rows for values. Suppose he finishes like this.

	Clubs	Diamonds	Hearts	Spades
Ace	KH	10D	5D	AC
Five	10S	10H	KD	AH
Ten	5C	AS	10C	5S
King	KS	AD	KC	5H

The player hits as follows: Clubs, 1; Diamonds, 2; Hearts, 0; Spades, 1; Total, 4. In values: Aces, 1; Fives, 0; Tens, 1; Kings, 2. Total 4.

That was average on both counts. But by keeping score of both, a player may find that he is better at guessing one type than the other. That may be ESP.

Card Sense

Some players who have tried this game have been amazed at the results. Six cards are used, one a face card, the rest all spots. They are shuffled and dealt in a row across the table, leaving about an inch of space between.

The player runs his hand back and forth along the row, keeping his thoughts focussed on the face card, like the K.D. After a while, he gains an impression of where the card is. Sometimes, his hand will lag or dip at a certain card, and when he slows the motion, the dip may become more noticeable.

That is the card the player turns up to see if it is the face card. Some people say they have a real ability at stopping on the right card, while others have no luck at all. At least it is worth a trial and anyone who hits two or three times out of six may very well be exercising ESP.

Elimination

This game is a form of ESP with a reverse twist. It is played with thirty-two cards taken from the pack at random, but there should be one special card in the group, such as the Ace of Spades. This is the card the player tries to eliminate by thinking "hot" and "cold."

The cards are shuffled and dealt in two packets of sixteen cards each, both face down. He tries to guess which half has the Ace and when his hunch gets strong, he lays that heap aside and eliminates the other heap by turning it face up and running through it. If his hunch is right, the Ace will not be there. So he picks up the Ace heap and deals it into two new piles of eight cards each.

Again, the player eliminates one half, and if his hunch is right, he deals the Ace heap into two piles of four. Another elimination follows and if it works, he deals two piles of two, and if he eliminates one of those, he is down to two cards which he lays side by side and tries to pick the Ace. When it reaches that stage, the game has lots of suspense, and the player has a right to be triumphant when he hits.

Esmeralda

Only twenty-six cards are used in this Solitaire. The thirteen Spades are shuffled in a packet called the Spade Stock and the thirteen Hearts are shuffled in a packet called the Heart Stock. Both are laid face down, side by side.

The player turns up the top card of the Spade stock, as the 4S to start a waste pile. Now, he deals cards from the Heart stock into another waste pile, as KH, 6H, 10H, 4H, stopping on the Four. Since this matches the 4S in value, both are removed. The player then deals again from the Spade stock into its waste pile, as AS, JS, 9S, 6S, 10S. Since the Ten matches the top card of the Heart waste pile, both are removed. That leaves the 6S and 6H showing on their respective piles, so they too are removed.

The player continues this process, dealing from either stock, hoping to match the other waste pile and work back until all are eliminated. At the finish of a deal, both waste piles can be turned down and dealt through again.

Playback

This is like Esmeralda, but with forty cards. The Spades and Clubs from Ace to Ten form a packet known as the Black Stock while the Hearts and Diamonds from Ace to Ten are the Red Stock. Deal from one, then the other, hoping to match a Red with a Black in value, and thus "play back" through the waste piles. Three deals are allowable.

Klondike

This game is practically the same as Canfield in the original version, with cards dealt singly from the stock and only one deal allowed. Since the game came into popularity about the time of the Klondike gold rush in 1897, it is very possible that Klondike is its correct name.

Gold Rush

This is standard Canfield or Klondike with one special feature. The player starts with the regulation tableau and begins dealing singly from the stock into a waste pile. As soon as a play can be made from the waste pile, the player has made a strike and that pile becomes a claim.

The next card dealt from the stock goes into a new

waste pile, which also becomes a claim when a card is played from it. Half a dozen claims may be established during the deal and the top card of each claim or waste pile is always available. This makes the game easier than Klondike while still retaining the restriction of a single deal through the stock.

Kingsley

This is simply Canfield or Klondike in reverse. The four Kings are used as foundations and are built down by suits, Queen, Jack, Ten, and so on to the Ace. On the tableau, cards are packed in alternate colors, but in upward sequence, as the 2D on AC or AS; the 4C on the 4D or 4H, the QS on the JH or JD. All other rules conform to Klondike or any form of Canfield.

La Parisienne
Two Packs

Old, but good, with a unique reserve feature. Four Aces are set in a row, one of each suit, as foundations to build up to Kings. Beneath that, four tableau cards are dealt face up, to form auxiliary piles. Below that, four Kings, one of each suit, as foundations for building down to Aces. Two more cards are then dealt face down to start the Reserve.

AD	AC	AH	AS	reserve
9S	6C	QD	7H	* *
KD	KC	KH	KS	cards

The player builds what he can from the tableau, the only build here being QD on KD. He deals four more cards face up on the tableau (including the gap left by the QD) and two more face down to the reserve. This continues through the double pack, building from the tableau when possible. Then the entire reserve of 32 cards is turned face up and any of its cards may be used in further builds.

When blocked, piles are gathered face up from right to left, beginning with the reserve, then the tableau piles. This stock is turned face down and dealt through as before. Four deals are allowable in all, as this is a difficult game.

Grand Duchess

Two Packs

This is virtually the same game as La Parisienne, but it it even harder. The reason is that only four tableau cards and two Reserve cards are dealt to start. The foundation rows must wait until Aces and Kings of different suits show up in the deal, when they are placed above and below the tableau, respectively.

Eight Mighty Monarchs

Two Packs

This game is started by placing any King face up on the table as the first in a row of eight tableau piles The pack is then shuffled and cards are dealt face up on the lone King. When an Ace appears, it is set as a foundation above the King and other Aces go in that same row. These foundations are to be built in ascending sequence clear up to King, but suits do not matter. Any Two can go on any Ace, and so on.

When a King appears in the deal, it is placed beside the first King. From then on, the cards are dealt face up on the second King, until a third King appears, when it becomes the next pile of the tableau and cards are dealt on it. This keeps on until there are eight piles, each with a King at the bottom.

Salic Law

Two Packs

The Queens are removed from the pack as totally ineligible. The game then preceeds exactly as described in Monarchs, but the foundations are built only as high as Jacks, who represent the eligible princes: while the Kings remain alone on their thrones as represented by the original tableau piles.

Golden Gate

Three Packs

All Aces form the top of the gate, the Kings, six to a side, are the uprights, and the doorway is composed of six columns of eight cards each, all face-up, overlapped to save space. Here is an illustration:

AS	AS	AS	AD	AD	AD	AH	AH	AH	AC	AC	AC
KD	3D	JH	9S	QH	10H		3S				KH
KD	JC	QC	3S	10D	QD		10C				KH
KD	9S	2S	JC	10S	6H		8C				KH
KS	4H	7D	10D	JS	4D		10S				KC
KS	5D	6H	2C	8S	2S		4C				KC
KS	JC	5S	4D	5S	QH		7C				KC
	9S	8D	2H	JD	3D		6D				
	7C	2D	QS	8S	2C		7D				

Cards from the tableau are built upward on the Ace foundations by suit, and downward on the King foundations by suit. In the illustration, the player would build the 2D on an AD, the QS on a Ks, the 2C on an AC. The 2H would be available for play on an AH, and the 3D on the 2D. That would make the 4D available for play on the 3D, and the QH on a KH.

In short, only the bottom cards of the tableau can be built, releasing the next card of its column. However, cards can not be transferred from one column to another, until a space is formed. Then, an available card from another column may be moved.

Only one such deal is allowable, but the player can shift cards back and forth on foundations. If an AH has been built up to the 6H, and a KH down to the 7H, the 6H moved on to the 7H, or vice versa.

Pearly Gates
Three Packs

Aces and Kings are placed in position as they appear while dealing the tableau, and the player begins working with those. The rest are placed when they appear during the deal of stock to waste pile.

Heavens Above
Three Packs

Another form of The Golden Gate, this Solitaire has just one variation that makes it easier. Aces and Kings are first placed as foundations in the shape of a gateway, but the tableau, consisting of the actual gates, is different. Instead of six columns of eight cards each, it has eight columns of six each.

Discard

This quickie has a simple tableau of four cards:

6D   8H   4S   QH

Any card lower in value than another of its suit is discarded, values running K-Q-J-10-9-8-7-6-5-4-3-2-A, as is usual in most Solitaires. In this game the 8H is discarded, leaving:

6D   4S   QH

Four more cards are dealt on the tableau row, as:

KD   10H   5C   6S

All suits are different, blocking play. Four more are dealt, with a result like this:

3D   10C   10D   9S

The 3D is discarded, showing KD. The 10D is discarded, showing 5C. The 5C is discarded, showing 4S. The 4S is discarded, making space which may be filled by any card. The KD is best, showing 6D, which is discarded, leaving space which is best filled by 9S. The 6S is discarded, leaving a blocked row:

9S   10C   KD   QH

Four more cards are dealt on the row and play continues, the goal being a row of Four Kings.

Aces High

This form of Discard is preferred by players who are accustomed to the usual rank of cards used in games other than Solitaire, namely: A-K-Q-J-10-9-8-7-6-5-4-3-2. It is played exactly like Discard, but since Aces are high, they are the best cards to move into spaces, and the player wins the game if the tableau finally contains a row of just four Aces.

Solitaire Piquet

So-called because a Piquet pack of thirty-two cards is used, with values running A-K-Q-J-10-9-8-7. Four cards are dealt in a face-up row; four more are dealt on those, and so on. After each deal of four, any Ace is removed and used to start a foundation row above the first card in the tableau. The next Ace goes above the second tableau card, and so on.

Builds are made on Aces in descending order, but to be built, a tableau card must be just below a foundation card of the same suit.

AC   QD   KS

JD   5H   QS   8S

The JD can not be built on the QD, but the QS can be built on the AS. After the whole pack is dealt, heaps are gathered, one on another, from right to left; the pack is turned over and cards are dealt on the row of four as before, with builds between deals.

When a foundation is completed from Ace down to Seven, it is removed and only three tableau heaps are dealt. Another completed suit reduces the tableau to two heaps, and finally to only one.

Amazons

This is an abridged version of the Piquet Solitaire. Aces and Kings are first removed, leaving only twenty-four cards, which are built in ascending sequence from Sevens, as Foundations, to Queens, who represent the Amazon warriors.

Storehouse

This famous Solitaire is easy to play, but hard to beat. The Aces are dealt in a face-up row as foundations. The pack is shuffled and four cards are dealt in a face-up row to start auxiliary piles. Thirteen cards are dealt face down, and this packet is turned face up at the left of the tableau, as the Storehouse:

					Found-ations
	AD	AC	AH	AS	
Store-	8C	JC	2D	10D	
6H					Auxil-iaries
house					

	Stock	Waste
	*	3D
	Pack	Pile

The remainder of the pack is set face down as a Stock, and its top card is dealt as a waste pile.

Builds are made on foundations in ascending sequence, Ace up to King, according to suits. Top card of Storehouse, any auxiliary pile, or waste pile, can be used to build.

Auxiliary piles may be packed in descending sequence, by alternating colors, from Storehouse, waste pile or another auxiliary. However, once a descending sequence has been formed, it can only be moved as a unit. JC - 10D - 9C - 8H as an overlapping sequence could only be moved on the QH or QD.

In the illustration, the 2D would be built on the AD, the 3D on the 2D. The 10D would be packed on the JH. One space would be filled by the 6H, showing another card on the Storehouse, which could be used to fill the other space. A new card would be dealt from stock to waste-pile, that card also being available for any play. After dealing through the stock, card by card, the waste pile is turned over as a stock, and can be dealt twice.

Deadly Deuces

This is Storehouse with the Twos, or Deuces, used as foundations instead of the Aces. Builds follow the usual ascending sequence, but run 2-3-4-5-6-7-8-9-10-J-Q-K-A, the Ace being the highest card, as is usual in many card games.

Warehouse

Identical to Storehouse, with one exception. The special pile of thirteen cards, in this case termed the Warehouse, must be used to fill spaces in the tableau. Such spaces can not be filled from the waste pile until the Warehouse is exhausted. Usually, a player prefers to fill such spaces from the Warehouse, but as the packet dwindles, there are times when he may want to fill from the waste pile instead. He can't in this game, which may make it a bit more difficult. Either Aces or Deuces may be used as foundations in Warehouse.

Dealer's Dozen

This variant can be applied to either Storehouse or Warehouse. It is exactly the same game, but only twelve cards are used in the special packet.

Devil's Own

Thirteen cards are dealt in a packet which is turned face up as a reserve. Four cards are then dealt in a face-up row as a tableau. Another card is dealt face up as the first of four foundations:

8S   4D   8C   JD   9H   Tableau
Reserve

   5H   Foundations

Top card of the reserve or any tableau pile may be built in ascending sequence on the foundation, but strictly by suit. Here, the player is ready to build Hearts in order 5-6-7-8-9-10-J-Q-K-A-2-3-4. Tableau cards may be packed from the reserve or among themselves in descending sequence, alternating in color, as 8C on 9H. As these form, they must be transferred in groups, as 9H - 8C going on to 10C or 10S. Spaces are filled from the reserve.

When play is blocked, cards are turned up by threes from the remainder of the pack, or stock, and used to form a waste pile, with its top card available for building or packing. As more foundation cards appear, they are placed in a row beside the first, and built up by suits. In this case, the cards would be the 5C, 5S and 5D.

Thirteen Up

Played like the Devil's Own, but with restriction on the waste pile removed, so it can be used to fill tableau spaces at any time.

10D	3D	10S	Space	AH
Reserve	2C	9H		
	AD	8S		
	KS			Tableau
5D	7H	QC	5S	Foundation

*

Stock

Waste

JS

Pile

The 9H - 8S were just move to 10S, leaving a space. Instead of filling same with 10D from the reserve, the player fills with JS from the waste pile, then moves the 10D on to the 9S.

Idiot's Delight

This is the Devil's Own with more restrictions removed, making it still greater fun for players who

love to have the game work out completely. The
player can spread the reserve pile, to see what is
coming next, which is not allowable in Devil's Own
or Thirteen Up. He can also move single cards or
portions of a tableau sequence if he wishes. In the
illustration given with Thirteen Up, he could move
the KS on to the AH. Or he could put AD - KS on
the 2S, if it happened to be in the tablaeu.

Square of Sixteen

An interesting Solitaire puzzle may be worked
with the Aces, Kings, Queens, and Jacks from a
standard pack. These are to be laid in four rows,
face up, so that one of each value (A, K, Q, J) appears in each row, vertically or horizontally.

Ten Different Rows

Having solved the Square of Sixteen, a further
problem may be presented, by calling for a square of
Aces and face cards, in which the horizontal, vertical and diagonal rows all differ as to suit and value.

Four in a Row

Another neat puzzler. Take any twelve cards from
the pack and deal them face down in rows, so that
there will be four cards in each horizontal row and
four in each vertical row.

The system is to deal nine cards in a square, then
deal one on the first card of the first row; another
on the second card of the second row; and the last
on the third card of the third row. All rows except
diagonals, will then contain exactly four cards.